COUNTRY GARDENS®

easy garden *projects*

200+ SIMPLE IDEAS FOR YOUR YARD, GARDEN & HOME

weldon**owen**

INTRODUCTION

accents & decor

hardscapes & growing accessories

plants & planters

four ways to captivate your senses

four ways to shape tiny trees

introduction

Growing things—digging in the dirt, planting, watering, weeding, cutting a bouquet of fresh flowers from your garden—is a deeply satisfying way to make your world (and life!) more wonderful. Gardening by its very nature is a personal pursuit, starting with where you live—the geography, soil, sunlight, plant material, and rainfall all have an impact on how your garden grows and what it looks like. And therein lies the beauty of *Easy Garden Projects*. This collection features a wide variety of simple things you can make or do to enhance your garden and home—whether you have an acre, a few pots on a balcony, or a single terrarium in a windowsill to cultivate. It might be crafting a homemade faux-stone planter or a potting bench made from reclaimed wood; repurposing vintage finds into a bird feeder; or making a living wreath for your front door. There is something here for every skill level and interest. No matter where you live and garden, *Easy Garden Projects* features fun ways to spend a weekend or just a few hours making something beautiful.

accents & decor

001 perfect a pussy willow wreath

Make a simple and striking wreath from pussy willow trimmings.

MATERIALS

48 pussy willow branches, each approximately 4 feet (1.2 m) long

Snips

Wire cutters

Paper-covered 26-gauge floral wire

6-inch (15-cm) diameter grapevine wreath base

STEP 1 Cut the pussy willow branches into 8 to 10-inch (20–25-cm) lengths (A). Save extra pieces to fill in openings that appear once branches have dried.

STEP 2 Gather six to eight branch pieces in one hand and form a fan-shape bundle (B).

STEP 3 Secure the bundle using a 5-inch (13-cm) length of paper-covered wire. Attach the bundle to the wreath base, twisting wire ends as tightly as possible to hold bundles in place (C).

STEP 4 Repeat steps 2 and 3 to cover the wreath base (D).

002 do a favor

Create pretty garden party favors with recycled glass jars and botanical and garden-theme postcards or book pages. Just slip the paper inside a large jar then insert a smaller jar filled with water and flowers (we used pink snapdragons).

TULIP TREE

Liriodendron tulipifera

The tulip tree is one of the shade trees of the states. Its clean-cut and tulip-like flowers in spring; its open out on leafless in winter. It grows rapidly and thrives in soft

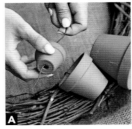

003 whip up a succulent wreath

Create a rustic all-season living wreath with just a few simple materials.

STEP 1 Gather a selection of pots. We used twelve 1½-inch (4-cm) pots, sixteen 2-inch (5-cm) pots, and twelve 3-inch (8-cm) pots. You can tie each individual pot to an 18-inch (46-cm) grapevine wreath, or work them into 5-foot (1.5-m) sections of cut crafts wire, wrapping six or seven pots with each section. Thread wire through the top first terra-cotta pot through the drainage hole and secure it to the wreath in an upright, plantable position. Add the next, angling pots topsy-turvy. Continue to form the arrangement you want (A). The more pots placed upright, the more room to plant, as upside down pots will be able to hold less weight.

STEP 2 Keep wrapping pots around the wreath until near the end of your wire section. Secure the wire end through the last wrapped pot. Wrap wire through this support a couple times, being careful to turn ends inward toward the wreath base (B).

STEP 3 Add a selection of succulents (C).

STEP 4 Hide the wire by covering with Spanish moss (D). Wrap moss around the root balls too, as it helps hold the succulents in their containers. Water weekly with a gentle spray or when moss feels dry.

004 serve up an artful arrangement

Choose a cake stand, purchase floral moss and foam, and gather succulents and roses to arrange this stunning display.

MATERIALS

Footed cake stand

Floral moss

Floral foam

Assorted flower and succulent blossoms

Heavy-gauge wire

STEP 1 Line the surface of a footed cake stand with moistened floral moss (A).

STEP 2 Soak a 3- or 4-inch (8- or 10-cm) cube of floral foam in water, then place it in the center of the cake stand on the moss. The saturated foam anchors the arrangement while keeping the flowers hydrated (B).

STEP 3 Trim the rose stems to 2 inches (5 cm) and insert them into the top of the foam cube, creating a tight cluster that overlaps the edges. Tuck succulent rosettes around the foam (C).

STEP 4 Continue to tuck in succulents (or small plants with soil removed) until the sides of the foam cube are concealed (D).

STEP 5 Clip succulents at the base and anchor around the flower stems (E). If necessary, insert heavy-gauge wire up through the center to secure so the rosettes face outward.

STEP 6 Continue to moisten the moss and foam for a long-lasting arrangement (F).

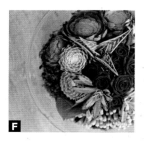

005 bring a wreath to life

Perfect for a door or fence, a living wreath transitions easily from season to season—thanks to a fresh profusion of blooming plants.

MATERIALS

- 1 pound (0.5 kg) sheet moss
- 16-inch (40-cm) wreath form
- Potting soil
- 24 small plants (try a combination of plants in 4-inch [10-cm] pots and even smaller plants in four-packs)
- Green floral wire

STEP 1 Soak the sheet moss in water; drain until it's damp and pliable. Line the wreath form with the sheet moss, green mossy side facing out, like fitting dough in a pie pan (A). Overlap pieces of moss and patch as you go.

STEP 2 Make sure the moss overlaps the upper edges of the form by about three fingers' width. Fill the form about three-fourths full with potting soil (B).

STEP 3 Arrange nursery pots on the soil. When happy with the design, take plants out of the pots one at a time and plant them (C).

STEP 4 Give the wreath a full look by planting the sides too. Poke holes through the sheet moss in three or four places around the sides of the form and carefully insert a plant in each hole (D).

STEP 5 Tuck overlapping edges of sheet moss around the crowns of plants (E). It holds plants in place until roots take hold and helps keep the soil from drying out.

STEP 6 Secure one end of the floral wire to the back of the wreath form. Wrap wire all around the wreath in a spiral pattern (F). Cut the wire and twist the end onto the form. Attach a short length of doubled wire to the form as a hanger; attach several more lengths to provide options for hanging orientation.

006 water living wreaths well

You can water a living wreath one of two ways: Lay it flat and pour water over it, or set it in a large shallow container of water until it feels heavy.

four ways to dress the door

Greet guests to your home in a fresh and beautiful way with a seasonal door dressing.

007 hang in the shade

Small shade-loving plants swirl around the 'Super Elfin' impatiens in this wreath. The ferns lend texture to the arrangement, while gold-and-green variegated ivies fill in bare spots and will trail around the wreath all summer. Use hairpins to hold the tendrils of ivy in place. Deadhead impatiens as they fade on this wreath to encourage more blooms and to keep the plants compact. (For basic instructions, see Bring a Wreath to Life #005.)

008 rake in autumn beauty

An aged-to-perfection rake head that has lost its handle makes an artful autumn sheaf. Simply tuck berry-laden twigs and vines into the hollow tube where the handle once was. We used Eastern red cedar (*Juniperus virginiana*) and a few strands of American bittersweet (*Celastrus scandens*) for an unexpected color combination. A wrapping and bow of baling twine adds a rustic final touch. NOTE: American bittersweet is native and not to be confused with the highly invasive Chinese or Oriental bittersweet that should not be planted.

009 round up pinecones & apples

This eye-catching wreath, made from heavy-gauge wire, mixes the gloss of polished apples and the spiky scales of pinecones. Simply skewer the apples onto the wire. Use additional wire to attach pinecones, then bend wire ends into hooks and connect them in a circle. To finish the wreath with country charm, tie on a bouquet of tickle-soft white pine boughs. For a dash more color, tuck in a few twigs of scarlet bittersweet—any red berries or crabapples will do.

010 create a circle of thyme

A kitchen garden wreath planted with herbs smells as good as it looks. This herb wreath contains spearmint, rosemary, and several varieties of thyme. Little violas add spots of color—you can toss the flowers in a salad too. An herb wreath will flourish in summer heat, and trimming off snippets will encourage the plants to grow. You can plant perennial herbs at the end of summer. (For basic instructions, see Bring a Wreath to Life #005.)

011 create a vertical garden

All you need are a few supplies from the hardware store, a vintage vent cover, plants, and potting soil.

MATERIALS

Vintage vent cover or frame

Spray paint and/or polyurethane

Red cedar and laths

Nails

Wire mesh

Snips

Coconut-fiber mat

Potting soil

Screws

Screwdriver or drill

Succulents

Decorative fencing or grate

Moss

Sturdy picture hooks

STEP 1 Prevent moisture damage by sealing the vent cover or frame with a coat of paint or polyurethane varnish. An old portrait frame or heating vent cover each work well to surround a vertical garden with character.

STEP 2 Use long-lasting red cedar and nails to make a box 4 to 5 inches (10–13 cm) deep that matches the dimensions of the frame. Back with laths for stability and drainage. Seal with polyurethane. Line the interior with wire mesh to hold soil in place (A).

STEP 3 Add the coconut-fiber mat, then fill with potting soil that includes a slow-release fertilizer (B). (Lightweight potting soil, as opposed to heavy garden loam, is essential for vertical gardens.)

STEP 4 Using screws and a screwdriver or drill, attach the prepared frame to the planting box (C).

STEP 5 Fill the framed mini garden with a collection of low-water plants. For eye-catching visual interest, mix contrasting textures and colors. Sedum with tiny green leaves sits beside the hefty foliage of blue-gray Echeveria (D).

STEP 6 Insert a short piece of decorative fencing or an old grate as an accent or shelf. Cover soil with moss. Hang the frame on a west- or south-facing wall with picture hooks.

012 frame your plants as works of art

Explore the variety of leaf shapes and colors in a piece of framed living art that showcases the beauty of botanicals at eye level. Silver-gray Echeveria anchors the lower half, while clusters of hens-and-chicks mingle with sedums and creeping thyme to create a tapestry of texture. (For basic instructions, see Create a Vertical Garden #011.)

013 shelve it

You don't have to go to all the fuss of planting a vertical garden inside a frame (see Create a Vertical Garden #011)—you can get a similar effect by arranging botanical displays on shelves made from backless 4-inch- (10-cm-) deep boxes hidden behind repainted vintage frames. Use a varied selection of potted succulents in and atop the boxes, and paint the frames punchy colors.

014 table it

Add depth to a cast-off table with an old frame. Mount a frame on the top, fill with potting soil, then plant an arrangement of succulents or other low-growing plants. (For basic instructions, see Create a Vertical Garden #011.)

015 wire up a trellis

Turn vintage wire fencing into a vine-taming pot trellis.

MATERIALS

Potted black-eyed Susan vine (*Thunbergia*)

20-inch- (50-cm-) diameter planter

Potting soil

6-foot- (1.8-m-) long section of ornamental wire fencing

Heavy-duty pliers

Bolt cutters or heavy-duty wire cutters

STEP 1 Remove your plant from its nursery pot and place it in the center of the planter. Fill in the gaps with potting soil.

STEP 2 Unroll the wire fencing, and use the pliers to straighten any bent tips and ends. Cut the fencing to the desired length (plus extra for fastening together the ends) by snipping the horizontal wires with bolt cutters (A). (For our 20-inch- [50-cm-] diameter pot, we cut a 65-inch [165-cm] length of fencing.)

STEP 3 Roll the fencing into a cylinder and insert it in the pot to check fit. Twist the cut ends of the horizontal wires over the wires on the opposite edge of the fencing, then crimp to secure (B). Trim excess length with bolt cutters.

STEP 4 Anchor the finished trellis in the pot around the plant and tease the vines around the wire supports.

016 light up the night

Add ambience to a garden or an outdoor living area by filling glass globes from light fixtures with bright, warm LED light strings.

MATERIALS

Three 11-foot (3.5-m), 30-light battery-operated LED light strings

24-gauge wire

Wire cutters

AA batteries

3 glass ceiling light globes (ours are 4-inch [10-cm], 6-inch [15-cm] and 7-inch- [18-cm-] diameter)

5½-inch- (14-cm-) diameter blue glazed pot

4-inch- (10-cm-) diameter green glazed pot

Old table lamp base

STEP 1 For each light string, cut a piece of wire to match its length. Twine the wire around the light string cable to make the strand more manageable when placing it inside a globe (A). Install AA batteries in the battery pack.

STEP 2 Tuck a strand of lights into a 7-inch- (18-cm-) diameter glass globe, bending and shaping the strand to fill the globe. Set the lights to switch on at dusk, and place the battery pack inside the 5½-inch (14-cm) pot (B). Turn the globe over and nestle it on top of the pot.

STEP 3 Thread a light string through the drainage hole of a 4-inch (10-cm) pot and into the 4-inch- (10-cm-)

diameter globe (C). Turn the pot upside down over the battery pack to conceal it, and set the globe on top of the inverted pot.

STEP 4 Fill a glass globe with a wired light set, then place it on the lamp base, tucking the battery pack inside the base. Place the trio of lights at a garden bed edge, in a patio corner, or where you want an unexpected hint of light.

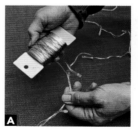

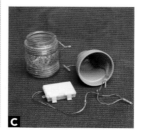

four ways to get your glow on

Add soft candlelight to your next garden party with these make-in-minutes accents crafted from what you have on hand or from favorite finds from vintage shops. Always be careful with open flame!

017 glow vintage

Finally, there's a use for all those mismatched glass light fixtures you've saved: They make wonderful votive candleholders. Fill a galvanized plant tray with sheet moss, insert the votive candles inside the upturned glass shades, and place the display on a flat surface to light up the night.

018 light up a basket

Metal baskets transform into lovely rustic outdoor chandeliers. Fill the bottom with a layer of green moss and insert pillar candles. Suspend the basket with three equal lengths of medium-weight sturdy rope evenly spaced around the basket perimeter. Hang above a dining table where it can cast its magical glow.

019 float flowers

Enjoy favorite garden flowers even after the sun has set. Fill a galvanized bucket with water and gently float a kaleidoscope of blossoms—and small bits of moss for filler—on the surface of the water, anchoring the arrangement with a single squat candle for a movable floral night-light.

020 light the way

If you have a box of canning jars gathering dust, clean them and put them to good use. Place a votive candle in each jar and repurpose them as hurricane lanterns. Attach a wire handle to hose clamps wrapped around the jars and suspend from a branch or shepherd's hook to softly light a path.

021 hang an air-plant chandelier

Brighten a spot, indoors or out, with jewel-tone air plants.

MATERIALS

Small needle-nose pliers

Approximately 13 feet (4 m) of 20- or 22-gauge beading or floral wire

7 large beads

One 10- to 12-inch- (25–30-cm-) diameter hanging basket

6 air plants, 5 small and 1 medium-size (we used *Tillandsia abdita* and *T. caput-medusae*)

quick garden tip

022 take care of air plants

Although the nickname suggests *Tillandsia* need only air to survive, like other tropical plants, they require light, water, and good air circulation. However, they are easy to care for and will happily move indoors during cold months.

STEP 1 Using the cutting edge of the pliers, cut a 2-foot (60-cm) length of wire, then thread a bead onto it (A). Create a spiral below the bead by grasping one end of the wire with the pliers tip, winding it loosely around the tip for several turns, then carefully sliding the pliers out. Shape the spiral as you like with your fingers.

STEP 2 To create a holder for an air plant, move your hand above the bead and wrap the wire gently around your index and middle fingers one or two turns, then slide your fingers out (B). Place a small air plant inside the space where your fingers were, with the base of the plant near the bead. Wind wire gently one more turn to hold the plant in place. Create another curve or spiral above or below the plant if you like. Repeat for all plants, except use a 3-foot (90-cm) length of wire and two beads for the medium-size air plant.

STEP 3 Remove the liner from the hanging basket, if it has one, and save it for another use. Flip the basket to hang upside down from its chains. Arrange the small plants around the outside rim of the basket, adjusting the wire length as you like (C). Hang the larger plant from the center of the basket. When pleased with the arrangement, wrap the ends of the wires on the basket three or four turns, then clip off any excess wire with the cutting edge of the pliers. Hang your air plant chandelier in an area of bright but indirect light—never in full sun.

STEP 4 To water the plants, take the chandelier down and carefully place it over a large bowl of tepid water, submerging the plants for 30 to 60 minutes (D). After watering, tip over each plant to drain excess water. Air plants love warm humidity, so during dry weather or if grown indoors, water them once or twice a week. Protect plants from high winds and temperatures lower than 50°F (10°C).

A

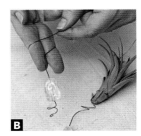

B

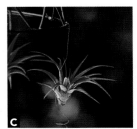

C

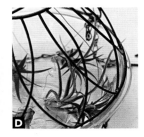

D

023 deliver storage

An old mailbox becomes a dry, convenient place to stash sunglasses or your garden journal. If you're a gardener prone to unexpected visitors, use the box to distribute plant lists or garden tour information. That's what we call first-class service.

LETTERS

024 put it on a pedestal

Brighten a shady spot with a planter atop a white birch-log pedestal.

MATERIALS

Drill and ½-inch (13-mm) drill bit

3 white birch logs

¼×6-inch (6×15-cm) rebar

Industrial-Strength Adhesive

Pea gravel (optional)

Low bowl planter and saucer

Potted plant (we used a fern)

STEP 1 Drill a 1-inch- (2.5-cm-) deep hole into the center of one end of each white birch log to support the rebar in the log (A). Add adhesive to the hole for added security.

STEP 2 Drive the rebar into position in the ground and slip the holes in the logs over the rebar, pushing down to secure and create a level surface. We added a layer of pea gravel between the soil and the logs to protect the wood from moisture (B).

STEP 3 Adhere the plant saucer to the top of the pedestal using industrial-strength adhesive (C). Wait 24 hours for the adhesive to set. Place the planted container on the saucer.

---

project tip

025 switch the birch

Instead of white birch logs, use fallen or pruned branches from your garden. Cut even lengths to the height you want, and bundle together. If branches are 1 inch (2.5 cm) in diameter, bundle five to seven branches of equal length together.

026 pack a cool kokedama

Literally "moss ball" in Japanese, these string gardens are a combination of two types of bonsai styles. Minimalist and modern, they add a natural touch to any space.

MATERIALS

Potting soil

Topsoil

Sphagnum peat moss

Perlite

Water

Plants

Mister

Natural sheet moss

Nylon twine

S-hooks

STEP 1 The day before you make a kokedama, mix the soil: three parts potting soil, two parts topsoil, one part sphagnum moss, and one part perlite. Add enough water to achieve a doughlike consistency, then soak the mixture, ideally for 24 hours. You should be able to make a ball with the soil by squeezing the moisture out of it.

STEP 2 Next, remove a plant from its pot and gently rub the soil away to expose the roots. Your goal is to make a round ball, so you'll need to reshape the root base (A).

STEP 3 Pack the soggy mix around the roots as if making a snowball (B). Add a little soil at a time, pressing the ball together and turning. You can set the plant on a surface, but you'll create a better ball shape if in your hands.

STEP 4 Soak or thoroughly mist several pieces of sheet moss (C) and apply to the ball, completely covering the soil. It's fine if the moss overlaps in places. Tuck the moss in around the crown of the plant so no soil is visible.

STEP 5 Wrap the ball with nylon twine (D). Tie a loop in one end, wrap the string around the ball and pass the other end through the loop, pulling it tight around the equator. Continue wrapping, securing the moss firmly in place, passing close to the crown of the plant and across the bottom. Wrap the ball several times to ensure the moss stays intact when you water the kokedama. Pull the twine tight and tie off the loose end near the top of the ball with a secure knot to finish.

STEP 6 Tie an additional string to the top of the ball for hanging. Attach an S-hook to the string to make it easy to hang and to remove the kokedama for watering.

027 go a round with dogwood

Woven into 12- and 18-inch- (30- and 46-cm-) diameter orbs, the colorful branches of red-twig and yellow-twig dogwood contrast beautifully with their surroundings.

MATERIALS

Ornamental dogwood branches (red: *Cornus alba, C. sericea,* and *C. stolonifera*; yellow: *C. sericea* 'Flaviramea')

Grapevines

Snips

18-gauge wire

Wire cutters

STEP 1 Gather red-twig or yellow-twig dogwood branches (A).

STEP 2 Cut grapevines and twist a length into a circle roughly the desired diameter of your sphere (B). Wrap and tuck the vine ends to hold them in place.

STEP 3 Make another circle of grapevine, the same size as the first, and fit the two circles together to form a perpendicular framework (C).

STEP 4 Use a piece of 18-gauge wire to secure the vine circles at each point where they meet. Twist and tuck in the wire ends (D).

STEP 5 Add lengths of vine to round the base for your sphere. Weave colorful dogwood branches over and under other branches and vines. Continue adding branches to the sphere, filling large gaps and tucking the ends in place (E).

STEP 6 Add as many branches as you wish to complete the sphere. Press on the sphere with your palms to round the shape as needed (F).

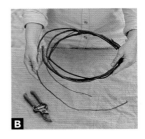
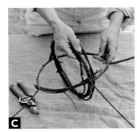

project tip

028 prune properly

If gathering dogwood branches by pruning, be sure it's the right time of year. Dogwood (and most other shrubs and trees) should ideally be pruned from late winter into early spring, when plants are dormant and it's easy to see among bare branches what needs to be pruned. Do the plant a favor and encourage growth by removing low-hanging branches that look dead or damaged, even if you're not going to use them for your orbs. Be careful not to damage the dogwood's sensitive bark, as wounds in the bark can invite fungus and parasites. Remove any excess growth from your selected branches so they'll be smooth for bending.

029 build a multipurpose tower

Terra-cotta pots provide the building blocks for this all-in-one planter, birdbath, and lantern.

MATERIALS

Paintbrush

Exterior primer and paint

12-inch- (30-cm-) diameter terra-cotta saucer

10-inch- (25-cm-) diameter tapered terra-cotta pot

18-inch- (46-cm-) diameter terra-cotta bowl

14-inch- (36-cm-) diameter tapered terra-cotta pot

Small rocks or pea gravel

Potting mix

Plants (we used Surfinia trailing petunia 'Rambling White,' *Lophospermum lofos* Compact White, and sweet alyssum 'Frosty Knight')

Large stones

Floating candles

STEP 1 Apply exterior primer to the outside of the pots; let dry overnight. Brush one or two coats of exterior paint on the pots; let dry thoroughly between coats (A).

STEP 2 Once you have determined your desired location, set up the pots in the intended configuration to see how they fit together as well as how the planter/lantern suits the site (B).

STEP 3 Turn the large tapered pot upside down; set it in place. Set the bowl on top of the large tapered pot. Fill the bottom of the bowl with rocks or gravel to facilitate drainage once the bowl is planted (C). Turn the small tapered pot upside down and set it in place inside the bowl on top of the rocks. Fill the bowl halfway with potting mix. Add plants, alternating petunias, lophos, and sweet alyssum. Fill in between the plants with potting mix. Water thoroughly.

STEP 4 Set the saucer on top of the small tapered pot. Fill the saucer with water (D). Add a few large stones if desired to provide a perch for birds or for decoration.

STEP 5 Add floating candles to the water, or skip the water and nestle LED lights into gravel to create a lantern after sunset. If using water, scatter a few blossoms across the surface for a romantic effect.

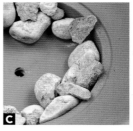

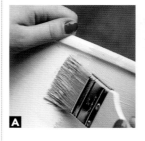

030 run for the border

Give your garden a custom look with edging that makes use of flea market finds, personal collections, or cast-off garden pots.

FRUIT BOXES (A) The colorfully labeled ends of wooden fruit crates bring color and eclectic style to the garden. Make boards more weather-worthy by sealing them with several coats of marine-grade polyurethane.

COOKIE CUTTERS (B) Use a nail and hammer or an awl to pierce the bottoms of metal cookie cutters, then use a small wood screw to secure each to the top of a painted or stained wooden stake.

FLOWER POTS (C) Surround a bed with terra-cotta pots in a range of sizes. To stabilize the pots, pack each with damp sand then turn it upside down and place it along the garden edge. Buy these garden icons for pennies, new or used, with or without collars.

LICENSE PLATES (D) Take pride in your home state. Salvaged license plates stand out as ornamental elements between plantings and landscape timbers. Tuck the slender profiles of license plates into place alongside existing plantings. Gently bend the plates to adapt them to curves.

031 sprout mushroom ornaments

Once they're stationed in the garden, these decorative concrete fungi will cure and harden over time, becoming more stonelike and developing an earthy patina as they're exposed to weather.

MATERIALS

Hand saw

Branches

Drill

Bowls or other mold shapes

Vegetable oil

2 plastic tubs

Sand

Waterproof gloves

Scoop

Concrete mix

Water

Bamboo stakes

STEP 1 To make stems for the mushrooms, saw sturdy branches of an even diameter into 10- to 12-inch (25–30-cm) lengths. Drill into the bottom of each branch, using a drill bit to make a hole sized to fit a bamboo stake (A).

STEP 2 Smear the inside of each bowl (or other mold) with a generous coat of vegetable oil; it will help the mold release easily from the concrete after it dries (B).

STEP 3 Fill one of the plastic tubs with sand; set aside. Wearing waterproof gloves, scoop dry concrete mix into the second plastic tub. Following the directions on the concrete mix bag, add water and blend to make a workable mixture the consistency of chunky peanut butter (C).

STEP 4 Place the bowls or molds in the tub of sand. Scoop prepared concrete into each bowl, filling it to the rim. Pat the wet concrete firmly to eliminate any air pockets. Work swiftly so you can complete the next step before the mixture hardens (D).

STEP 5 Push a stem into the concrete-filled bowl, drilled end facing out. As you press the branch 1 to 2 inches (2.5–5 cm) deep, the wet concrete will rise a bit and embrace it (E).

STEP 6 Set the tub of sand with the bowls in a shady place for 24 to 48 hours. Once hard, slide each mushroom out of its bowl (F).

STEP 7 Insert a bamboo stake into the hole of the mushroom stem (G). Choose a spot to display the ornament in the garden, and push the stake into the ground to hold the mushroom in place.

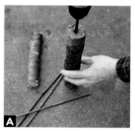
A

B

C

D

E

F

G

032 make a birdbath planter

An elegant combo of succulents in a sleek container shows these plants to their best advantage, and a drill in the hands of a patient do-it-yourselfer creates the sharp drainage the plants need to thrive.

MATERIALS

Lightweight two-piece terra-cotta or stoneware birdbath (without a locking top)

Masking tape

Water

Drill with ³⁄₁₆- and ½-inch (5-mm and 13-mm) carbide-tip ceramic drill bits

One 3-foot (90-cm) length of ⅜- or ½-inch (1-cm or 1.25-cm) steel rebar

Pea gravel

Coordinating pot with a ½-inch (1.25-cm) or larger drainage hole at the center

Potting soil for cacti and succulents

12 to 15 assorted small succulent plants

STEP 1 Place the birdbath bowl on the ground and center an X of masking tape on it. Add a small amount of water, approximately ¼ inch (6 mm) deep, to the center of the bowl to keep the bit and the bowl cool during drilling. Starting with the ³⁄₁₆-inch (5-mm) bit, carefully begin to drill in the center of the birdbath bowl. Go slowly and be patient—the small bit will need to break through the surface of the bowl and create a pilot hole for the larger bit. Do not push downward on the drill; allow the bit to do the work. Continue to drill with the small bit to a depth of ⅛ inch (3 mm) (A).

STEP 2 Switch to the larger drill bit and drill into the pilot hole. (Patience is important—depending on the thickness and type of material, total drilling time can be an hour or more.) While drilling with the larger bit, occasionally tilt the drill very slightly side to side to bite into the material. Protect the drill motor by taking intermittent breaks to allow it to cool down. When the bit begins to break through, the water will slowly drain; continue adding a small amount of water to keep the bit cool until the hole is completely drilled through (B).

STEP 3 Set the base of the birdbath in a sunny garden spot and place the drilled bowl on top. Slide the rebar through the drilled hole, pushing down into the garden soil to anchor the birdbath (C). Leave 3 to 4 inches (8–10 cm) of rebar sticking up through the bowl.

STEP 4 Spread a thin layer of pea gravel in the bowl. Place the coordinating pot on the gravel, sliding the pot's drainage hole over the protruding rebar (D).

STEP 5 Add potting soil to the pot and the birdbath bowl, then plant the succulents (E). Alternate trailing and mounding plants for the best appearance. Allow room for growth between plants.

STEP 6 Sprinkle pea gravel over the soil between the plants—to act as mulch, reduce erosion, and give the planting a finished look (F). Gently water the plants. In the absence of rain, water the planter every 10 to 14 days.

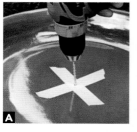

033 put a fire on

A small handmade fire bowl brings ambience and warmth to an outdoor setting.

MATERIALS

Dust mask

Waterproof gloves

White cement

Quartz sand

Perlite

Tub for mixing concrete

Water

Plastic trowel

12- and 16-inch- (30- and 40-cm-) diameter plastic planters

Vegetable oil spray

Sheet plastic

Metal file

Fire-safe decorative stones

Solid-gel fuel

project tip

034 play it fire-safe

Be sure to use fire-safe stones from a fireplace store (ordinary rocks might contain air pockets and moisture that cause them to burst). Don't use the fire bowl on a wood deck—and keep it away from dry leaves and sticks.

STEP 1 Wearing a dust mask and gloves, blend equal parts white cement, quartz sand, and perlite in a large tub. Slowly add water, and mix the concrete with a plastic trowel to form a consistency of soft dough that holds its form when squeezed into a handful (A).

STEP 2 Prepare the planters by spraying vegetable oil on the inside of the large one and the outside of the small one (B).

STEP 3 Working quickly, press the prepared concrete into the large planter, roughly forming a bowl shape approximately 2 inches (5 cm) thick (C).

STEP 4 Press the small planter firmly into the concrete; push hard to shape and smooth the inside of the fire bowl. Leave the small planter in place 2 to 3 minutes, then push down and rotate back and forth repeatedly to release. Repeat this process every few minutes until the concrete begins to set and hold its shape. Remove the small planter (D).

STEP 5 Use the trowel handle to form a drainage hole in the bottom of the concrete bowl. Leave the tool in place a few minutes until the concrete has set; remove (E). Cover the concrete bowl with a sheet of plastic; let cure for three days before moving it.

STEP 6 When cured, remove the plastic, carefully turn over the large plastic planter, and tip out the concrete bowl. Wrap the concrete bowl in the sheet of plastic, and allow it to cure in a shaded place for three weeks. When hard and dry, file top edge of bowl smooth (F).

STEP 7 Fill the concrete bowl with fire-safe decorative stones. Tuck cans of solid-gel fuel among the stones, using one, two, or three cans of fuel—the more cans of fuel, the hotter the fire. NOTE: Before using, check local fire safety ordinances.

A

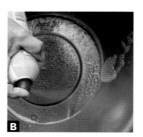
B

C

D

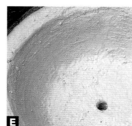
E

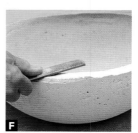
F

035 assemble a succulent centerpiece

Style happens on a patio table with the simplest of materials and coolest of plants.

MATERIALS

Adhesive felt protective discs

Stone or marble slab remnant

PVC fittings in assorted sizes and styles

Pebbles

4-inch- (10-cm-) diameter glass hurricane

Pillar or votive candles

Succulents

STEP 1 Place adhesive felt discs on the bottom of the marble slab to protect your tabletop, then set the marble in place on the table.

STEP 2 Position the largest PVC segment (ours is a 5-inch [13-cm] diameter) on the marble slab and fill with small pebbles. Place a glass hurricane (ours is 4-inch [10-cm] diameter) inside and drop in a pillar or votive candle.

STEP 3 Arrange five or six smaller PVC fittings in different sizes around the large one. To support the plants, fill the bottom of the PVC segments with pebbles to keep the succulents even with the top of the tube. Place succulents in nursery pots into the PVC fittings with matching diameters.

STEP 4 Scatter large pebbles around the arrangement. To water, remove plants from pots, water, and allow to drain thoroughly before returning to their holders.

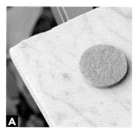

036 shine on with a sunburst

Hang this wall art for a sunny outlook in any weather.

MATERIALS

Exterior paint

Paintbrush

Twelve 12-inch (30-cm) wooden stakes

Spar urethane (optional)

Large nail or awl

Hammer

Decorative metal plate

1-inch (2.5-cm) wood screws

Drill

Picture hanger or wire

STEP 1 Apply a coat of exterior paint to the wooden stakes; let dry overnight. Brush on a second coat of paint or, if you prefer, a coat of exterior spar urethane; let dry (A).

STEP 2 Use a large nail or awl and hammer to make guide holes in the metal plate to fasten the stakes (B). Arrange the wooden stakes in a sunburst pattern, centering the guide holes in the metal plate over the wood stakes.

STEP 3 Screw through a guide hole and into a wooden stake; repeat to fasten all stakes to the plate (C). To prevent the stakes from pivoting, you may choose to add a second round of screws, positioning the screws about 1 inch (2.5 cm) from the first round.

STEP 4 Add a hanger to the back of the sunburst. Our plate came with a small hanger—we added a larger loop of wire to make hanging easy.

037 squash it

Cut off the tops of sturdy butternut
squash (about one-fourth of each
whole squash). Scoop out the flesh,
add a little water, and insert bold dahlia,
sunflower, or zinnia blooms for super-
easy, super-sweet bouquets.

038 add iron accents

Salvaged pieces of decorative iron added to garden planters enhance visual interest and give climbing plants something to cling to.

FENCING (A) Salvaged iron fence pieces create a unique tepee trellis. Bright pink and chartreuse colors offset the dark fence pieces. *Salvia × jamensis* 'La Siesta' and 'Saratoga Lime' Nicotiana peek through the trellis while 'White Palace' Lobelia, Lobelia 'Riviera Lilac,' and 'Colorsplash' petunia with variegated leaves soften the edges of the pot.

WIRE SHELF (B) A wire shelf piece becomes the vertical element of this window box. As the ivy fills in, the form will become completely covered and lush. Variegated *Helichrysum*, 'Sun Chimes' *Diascia*, English ivy, dahlia, and 'White Palace' Lobelia complement the color of the window box.

IRON LANTERN (C) A simple iron lantern takes on a new light as a lush potted garden ornament. Fragrant thyme is the centerpiece, while *Tweedia caerulea* vines spiral up the lantern's frame and *Nierembergia caerulea* 'Mont Blanc' fills in. For a romantic glow, substitute a pillar candle in the center for the *Nierembergia caerulea*.

039 display nature

Inspired by the art found in nature, this wall-mounted frame provides a place to showcase a collection of textural and beautiful botanical objects.

MATERIALS

1×2 wood boards

¾-inch (2-cm) nails

Hammer

¼-inch (6-mm) plywood

Wood glue

1-inch (2.5-cm) No. 6 wood screws

Drill and screw bit

Tape measure

⅜×2 wood boards

Stain/sealer

Brush

Two small D-ring picture hangers

Construction adhesive

Caulking gun

Natural materials: pinecones, seedpods, birch branches, moss, horsetail grass, bark

STEP 1 Cut the 1×2 boards to make a frame. Use nails to assemble the outer frame (A).

STEP 2 Cut plywood to fit the back of the frame. To secure the plywood to the frame, apply a bead of wood glue to the back edges of the frame, then fasten the plywood in place using screws (B).

STEP 3 Measure and cut small boards for compartment dividers. Secure dividers by applying a bead of wood glue to the bottom edge of each divider. Use nails to secure dividers (C). Let glue dry overnight.

STEP 4 Apply stain/sealer over frame and compartments (D). Let dry overnight. Brush on a second coat.

STEP 5 Attach picture hangers to the frame back for hanging. Fill each compartment with natural materials. Use dabs of construction adhesive to secure the objects (E). Let adhesive dry overnight before mounting the frame on a wall, fence, or other vertical surface.

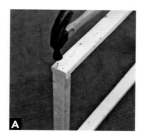

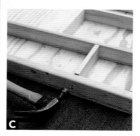

project tip

040 play with nature themes

A forage through the woods isn't the only way to go create a cherished display like the one featured here. Take a look at other precious collections, such as pressed or dried flowers, or perhaps a collection of seashells or sea glass. Once you decide on a theme, follow the steps above and you'll have a personalized keepsake or gift that keeps on giving through the seasons.

four spring baskets from vintage finds

Celebrate spring with bunches of fragrant flowers stuffed into one-of-a-kind baskets cleverly crafted from salvaged objects.

041 settle a spat

Recycle Victorian-era spats—often found at antiques stores. Sew new buttons to a spat. Insert a 3-inch- (8-cm-) wide container into the upturned spat. Tighten the spat to hold the pot in place. Tuck floral foam into a plastic bag, slip it into the container, and arrange flowers, such as delicate tulips. Add a ribbon to the spat's leather strap.

042 pretty up a tool

Slip a ribbon through a few blades of a well-worn meat grinder (if you spy a sharp edge, file it down) and line the container with sheet moss. Drop an old glass or jar inside (or use floral foam in a plastic bag) to hold flowers, such as these raspberry and white ranunculus, chartreuse viburnum, and shell-pink apple blossoms.

043 light a bouquet

Line a basket-style industrial light fixture with sheet moss. Thread a ribbon through two bolts and a washer to create a draw cord that allows for tightening the hanging loop, then tie the ribbon ends to the fixture sides. Tuck in blooms such as hyacinth, forsythia, and tulips.

044 finesse a funnel

Tie a ribbon to the handle of an old funnel; hang the funnel from a doorknob. Plug the spout with a cast-off cork. Cut floral foam to fit the funnel body and soak in water until saturated. Slip it into a plastic bag before tucking into the funnel. Add flowers.

045 go garden to table

Serve up a succulent plant display in a wooden patio table.

MATERIALS

Wooden outdoor table with slat construction

2 galvanized-steel drywaller's pans

Measuring tape or ruler

Eye and ear protection

Jigsaw

Drill and ⅜-inch (10-mm) drill bit

12 hardy succulent plants in small pots (*Sempervivum spp.* and trailing *Sedum spp.*)

Potting soil formulated for cacti and succulents

STEP 1 Assemble the table according to directions. Turn one of the drywaller's pans over and align the long edge of the pan evenly with the edge of the table's center support section. Use a pencil to trace the long edge of the pan that is opposite the center support—this marks the width of the top of the pan (A).

STEP 2 The goal is to cut a hole in the table that is smaller than the top of the pan so it can drop partway into the opening. Measure at least ½ inch (1.25 cm) inside the original pencil mark to create a cutting line (B). The edge of the center support will be the cutting line for the opposite side—the pan will drop in between them. Check measurements carefully, and avoid cutting through hardware under the table.

STEP 3 Wearing eye and ear protection, start at one end of the cutting line drawn in Step 2, slip the jigsaw blade between the slats, and start cutting directly on the line. Use firm even pressure to saw straight through your cutting line and the slats (C).

STEP 4 Saw the opposite side of the hole, using the edge of the center support as your cutting line, being careful not to over-cut. Repeat steps 1 to 4 for the other side (D).

STEP 5 Drill evenly spaced drainage holes into the bottom of both drywaller's pans with the ⅜-inch (10-mm) bit. Be patient—it will take a while to bore through the pan (E). Plant the succulents, adding potting soil as needed, then drop the planted pans into the openings.

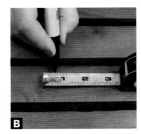

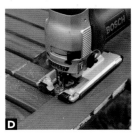

 project tip

046 make your table multitask

There's a bonus: Now that the table can hold standard drywaller's pans, you can pop in all kinds of things. Pick up a couple of extra pans and use them to hold ice for drinks, napkins and flatware, or a floral arrangement.

047 build a house of wires

This miniature house and its leafy garden are perfectly sized for an outdoor tabletop.

MATERIALS

Semitransparent weatherproofing wood stain

Paintbrush

Wooden crate

Drill

End snips

Wire garden edging panels (long enough to extend the length of the crate on two sides)

2 small wire garden trellises (each wide enough to extend the width of the crate)

Needle-nose pliers

24-gauge wire

20-foot (6-m) roll of wire scroll-top edging

Spray paint (we used a coral shade)

Potting mix

Plants: Golden moss, *Dichondra* 'Silver Falls,' creeping wire vine, Beth's lace flower vine, *Pilea* 'Aqua Marine'

STEP 1 Apply a light coat of wood stain/sealer to the wooden crate; let dry for two hours. Repeat with another coat (A); let dry for 72 hours before planting the crate. Drill one or two holes in the bottom of the crate for drainage.

STEP 2 Using end snips, cut and bend the wire edging panels as needed to make "walls" for a rectangular garden house that will fit in the wooden crate, adding small trellises at the front and back (B). The stakes, or legs, of the edging (and trellises) will anchor the structure in the planter.

STEP 3 Using needle-nose pliers, twist 1-inch (2.5-cm) bits of wire to join and secure the wire edging walls (C).

STEP 4 Use the scroll-top edging to make a roof for the house. Unroll the edging. Cut a length for each side of the roof and flatten the pieces (D). Bend the scroll tops of each section upward to form a roof peak. Place roof sections on the walls, joining the roof peaks together. Bend and cut the legs on the roof sections to connect them to the walls. Twist 1-inch (2.5-cm) wire as needed to secure the structure.

STEP 5 Spray-paint the wire house (E); let paint dry for two hours.

STEP 6 Fill the crate with potting mix. Tuck in the plants and water thoroughly (F). Stand the wire garden house in the planter and gently tease the vines to climb up the wires.

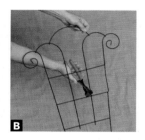

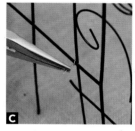

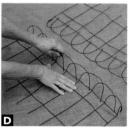

project tip

048 consider climbing plants

Creeping wire vine (*Muehlenbeckia*) works well for this planter. Other tiny ground covers or creeping plants can be trained up the wires of the house to form verdant walls.

049 lay an outdoor rug

This idea was inspired by the traditions of ancient Romans and Victorians who painstaking developed pebble mosaic techniques to create intricate courtyard floors and decorative paths.

MATERIALS

Tape measure

Stakes

String

Shovel

Crushed gravel

Coarse sand

Bricks and half bricks

Square cobbles

Square and crescent pavers

Green and ivory beach pebbles

STEP 1 Sketch your idea on paper, then measure the site for your rug. Use stakes and string to mark guidelines for the excavation. Dig out the area to a depth of 6 to 8 inches (15–20 cm), depending on your climate (see Dig Deep #050, below). Prepare a well-draining base for the rug with layers of gravel covered by sand (A). Mound the center of the excavation—slightly and gradually—to facilitate drainage.

STEP 2 Roughly lay out the largest stones to ensure components will fit. We used bricks and square cobbles for the perimeter, and half bricks and square pavers for the interior frame. Remeasure the perimeter and determine whether any additional materials are needed. Lay the rug frame, fitting pieces snugly in place (B).

STEP 3 Set the crescent pavers in place. Add a layer of gravel around the perimeter where the beach pebbles will be placed. The gravel will bring the pebbles to the same level as the rest of the rug components.

STEP 4 Finish laying the rug by filling in with beach pebbles. Stand the stones on their sides and fit them together as tightly as possible (C). This step requires some patience and puzzle-solving. If you wish, fill any gaps with tiny pebbles, pea gravel, or sand.

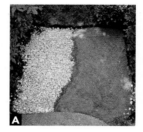

project tip

050 dig deep for a foundation

To excavate for the rug, we cleared a 50-square-inch (320-sq-cm) area, removing sod and soil to a depth of 8 inches (20 cm). In a cold-climate where freeze-thaw cycles can cause hardscape materials to shift and heave, a well-draining base requires a 4-inch (10-cm) layer of crushed gravel topped with a 2-inch (5-cm) layer of sand. In a warm climate, lay a 4-inch (10-cm) base: 2 inches (5 cm) of gravel plus 2 inches (5 cm) of sand. Allow enough depth to accommodate the bricks or pavers, keeping in mind that the rug will settle over time.

051 stencil stepping stones

Make way for a garden walk that includes intriguing signature artwork.

MATERIALS

Stencil

Concrete steppers (available at building supply stores)

Earth-tone outdoor spray paints

Newsprint

Pea gravel

STEP 1 Using a ready-made stencil that matches the size of the stepper, apply several earthy hues of outdoor spray paint following the stencil manufacturer's instructions. Apply each color separately, moving the stencil slightly after adding a color to give the stenciled image an illusion of depth. (NOTE: We used a various fossil pattern stencils, available online, and dark gray, light gray, and light brown spray paint.)

STEP 2 After applying the final color, blot the wet paint with a crumpled piece of newsprint to create an aged effect.

STEP 3 Set the stepping-stones where you want to create a pathway. Space them for a comfortable stride, about 2 feet (60 cm) apart. To place a stepper in a lawn, use a spade to cut around its perimeter. Dig under and lift out each circle of turf. Excavate to the depth of the stepper plus 1 inch (2.5 cm). Cover the bottom of the excavation with a 1-inch (2.5-cm) layer of pea gravel to aid drainage.

052 fall for a mini pot wreath

Premade grapevine wreaths are textural accents that you can easily dress up for the season. For an autumnal wreath, tuck in dried hydrangea blooms, bittersweet, and other seasonal flora. Wire miniature terra-cotta pots at various angles around the grapevine.

053 fashion a fountain

Create a spa-like atmosphere with a negative-edge fountain bubbling with calming waters.

MATERIALS

12-inch (30-cm) planter bowl with drainage hole in the center

Silicone sealer

Metal can lid

Waterproof adhesive

6 terra-cotta pot feet

Adjustable 100- to 170-gallon-per-hour (380–645-Lph) fountain pump

6 inches (15 cm) ½-inch (1.25-cm) ID (inside diameter) vinyl tubing

11-inch- (28-cm-) diameter metal splatter screen

Hacksaw and scissors

8-inch (20-cm) tapered planter with drainage hole in the center

Plumbers putty

Polished stones

STEP 1 Seal the drainage hole in the planter bowl by spreading a layer of silicone sealer around it. Lay a clean can lid (such as from a soup can) on top of the sealer and press down. Add another layer of sealer around the edge of the can lid (A). Let the sealer dry completely.

STEP 2 Place waterproof adhesive on one side of a pot foot and set a second pot foot on top of it. Repeat, gluing remaining pot feet together in pairs (B). Let dry completely.

STEP 3 Adjust the fountain pump to three-fourths of its maximum speed. Attach the vinyl tubing to the pump and set it in the center of the bowl. Place the stacked pot feet around it (C).

STEP 4 Cut the handle off the splatter screen with a hacksaw. Using scissors, carefully puncture a hole in the center of the splatter screen, enlarging it so the vinyl tubing fits through (D).

STEP 5 Place the splatter screen over the tubing and into the bowl, resting it on the stacked pot feet. Allow the pump cord to exit through a gap and over the bowl rim (E).

STEP 6 Place the tapered pot on the splatter lid, threading the vinyl tubing through the pot drainage hole. Center the tapered pot in the bowl and make sure the tubing stands straight up. Work a handful of plumbers putty with your hands until it is soft, then press it firmly around the vinyl tubing and the drainage hole, creating a seal to prevent water seeping through the drainage hole (F).

STEP 7 Move the fountain to desired location. Distribute the stones on the splatter screen around the base of tapered pot, completely covering the screen. Make sure the top container is level, the plumbers putty seal is tight, and the cord is hidden at the back of the fountain. Fill top container completely with water and pour water in the bottom bowl to just below the stones. Turn on the pump. Add water, if needed, to keep the top container overflowing freely.

A

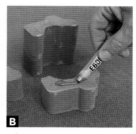
B

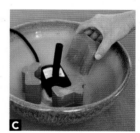
C

D

E

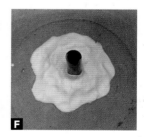
F

054 pebble your pavers

A ready-made concrete disk forms a durable base to embellish with a mosaic stone pattern.

MATERIALS

14-inch- (36-cm-) diameter concrete stepper

18×18-inch (46×46-cm) plywood

½- to 1-inch (1.25–2.5-cm) smooth pebbles

Waterproof gloves

Dust mask

Type S mason (mortar) mix

Water

Mixing bowl

Scoop

Plastic trowel

Plastic spatula

Tiling sponge

Sheet plastic

STEP 1 Draw around the concrete stepper on the plywood to make a guide for your design. Lay out the pebbles in a pleasing pattern on the plywood, contrasting sizes and colors (A). Fit the pebbles together like puzzle pieces, flattest side up.

STEP 2 Wearing gloves and a dust mask, prepare the mortar: Scoop 3 cups (1.5 kg) of mortar mix in the bowl and gradually stir in enough water to form a stiff consistency, comparable to peanut butter (B). If the mortar is too thin, add more dry mix; if too thick, add more water.

STEP 3 Use the trowel to apply mortar about ½ inch (1.25 cm) thick in the center of a concrete stepper. Start pressing pebbles into place, transferring the design from the plywood to the stepper (C). Mortar will fill in between pebbles to hold them in place.

STEP 4 Complete the process of pressing the pebbles into place within 30 to 45 minutes, before the mortar starts to set. Lay the plywood on top of the pebbles and press firmly to level the surface of the stepper (D). Use the spatula to press mortar between pebbles as needed to hold them firmly in place.

STEP 5 With a damp tiling sponge, gently wipe off excess mortar, rinsing the sponge frequently in clean water (E). Repeat the process until the last film of mortar has been removed from the surface of the stones. Avoid over-wetting the mortar, which would weaken the cement and the integrity of the mosaic. Rinse all tools as soon as possible after working with mortar.

STEP 6 Cover the stepper with a sheet of plastic for at least 48 hours, while it begins curing (E). Do not stand or walk on the stepper until it has fully cured, about three or four weeks.

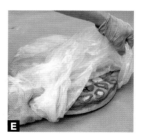

project tip

055 space out pavers

To make a path with pavers, set them in place. (See Step 3 of Stencil Stepping Stones #051 for more details on how to comfortably space them.) Excavate holes to paver depth plus 1 inch (2.5 cm). Fill the bottom of the hole with 1 inch (2.5 cm) of pea gravel to aid drainage, then top with a paver.

056 get some privacy

This colorful outdoor accent doubles as a clever way to block a view.

MATERIALS

Spray paint appropriate for PVC

Two 8-foot (2.5-m) lengths of ½-inch (1.25-cm) PVC pipe

Two 4-foot (1.2-m) lengths of ½-inch (1.25-cm) PVC pipe

Two ½-inch (1.25-cm) PVC elbows

4×7-foot (1.2×2-m) washable rod-pocket curtain panel

Scissors

Super Glue

Two 4 to 6-foot (1.2–1.8-m) lengths of ½-inch (1.25-cm) rebar

Small sledgehammer

STEP 1 Spray-paint the PVC elbows, and one 4-foot (1.2-m) length and both 8-foot (2.5-m) lengths of the PVC pipe (A). Allow them to dry completely, then spray a second coat.

STEP 2 To create the frame for the curtain panel, slide the painted 4-foot (1.2-m) length of PVC through the rod pocket of the curtain panel. Attach elbows at each end, and then attach 8-foot (2.5-m) lengths to the elbows (B).

STEP 3 At the bottom of the curtain panel, cut a small vertical slit in the hem at one end. Slide the unpainted 4-foot (1.2-m) length of PVC pipe into the hem to weight the curtain (C).

STEP 4 Tuck the PVC pipe completely inside the curtain hem and seal the opening closed with Super Glue (D); allow to dry.

STEP 5 Hold the framed curtain panel in its intended location (with assistance) to determine where to place the rebar. Use the sledgehammer to pound the rebar into the ground at least 1 foot (30 cm) deep (E). Keep the rebar vertical. Slide each side of the pipe frame over the pieces of rebar. If the curtain panel does not stand straight, adjust the rebar to vertical and space correctly.

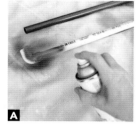
A

B

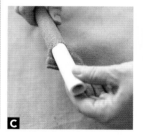
C

D

E

project tip

057 plant your privacy

For more enduring seclusion, consider installing a living wall as a privacy screen. Place a lattice wall, for example, and incorporate vining plants like ivies or Morning Glories to fill in the gaps as they grow, providing shade and privacy. Another option is planting a wall of bamboo to conceal your private oasis. Beware: Many plants that provide coverage are also highly invasive species. These plants can take over your and your neighbor's yard, so check with them first and consult an expert landscaper before committing to the project. If planting in the ground is an issue, vining plants will still overgrow even if contained to a pot.

058 display garden glass

Colored glass bottles of various shapes and sizes, inverted atop garden stakes, prove as eye-catching as flowers while providing eye protection as well. While boosting the appeal of flowerbeds, the clever caps prevent dangerous pokes when you're working among the blossoms.

059 circle 'round the seasons

Celebrate the beauty of plants year-round with an easy-change wreath.

MATERIALS

Floral wire

Six small fiber pots

Large grapevine wreath

Hot-glue gun and
   glue stick

Dried craft moss

Six plants in 2-inch
   (5-cm) pots

STEP 1 Thread floral wire through each fiber pot (A). Gently press the wire against the interior of each pot, creating space to insert the nursery container.

STEP 2 Use the floral wire to attach each fiber pot to the grapevine wreath (B). Create an eye-pleasing asymmetry by grouping the pots on one section of the wreath.

STEP 3 Hot-glue dried moss to the wreath around the pots (C). Glue only small portions at a time for a natural look.

STEP 4 Place miniature plants, still in nursery pots, in the fiber pots (D).

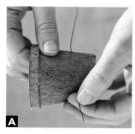

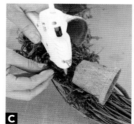

`project tip`

060 make it mini

Choose tiny plants for these pots, such as mini African violets, succulents, or even wee poinsettias that can be switched out with ease as seasons change. To water, remove plants from the fiber pots and soak in 1 inch (2.5 cm) of water for 30 minutes, then pop back into the fiber pots. For a fun firefly glow, add a string of battery-operated micro lights to the wreath.

hardscapes
& growing accessories

061 set up a germination station

Organize a space for starting seeds and wintering plants indoors.

MATERIALS

48×72×18-inch (120×185×46-cm) five-tier chrome-finish shelving unit

Four 4-inch (10-cm) industrial casters

Waterproof trays

Seed-starting soilless mix

Seed-starting trays and domes

Seeds

King-size heating pad

Two 4-foot (1.2-m) shop light fixtures

Four 40-watt fluorescent bulbs (2 warm; 2 cool white)

Electrical timer

STEP 1 Assemble the shelving unit. Place waterproof trays on shelves. Fill the seed-starting trays with the soilless mix; plant seeds. Place seed-starting trays in waterproof trays. Cover with the clear plastic dome to retain moisture. A heating pad, turned to a low setting, placed under the seed-starting tray creates gentle bottom heat that speeds sprouting of seeds (A).

STEP 2 Outfit both light fixtures with bulbs and suspend them from the bottom of two shelves. Adjust the fixture chains so the lights hang 3 to 4 inches (8–10 cm) above the seedlings (B). As the plants grow taller, raise the lights to maintain the same gap between the lights and plants. Use a timer to turn the lights on and off and to ensure that the seedlings receive 14 to 16 hours of light daily.

STEP 3 Line each shelf or seed-starting flat with a watertight tray to prevent moisture from dripping onto the floor and getting onto the heating pad. Water seeds and seedlings from the bottom to promote healthy plants and to keep the seed-starting mix damp but not wet (C).

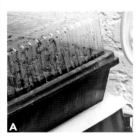
A

B

C

062 keep plants warm with cold frames

For our cold frames, we used barnwood for the straight sides and tin for the curved and pointed ends. You can also use salvaged or purchased wood and paint it or leave it untreated.

MATERIALS

Saw and hacksaw

Nontreated cypress, cedar, or other wood for sides

Tape measure

Salvaged window

3 feet (1 m) of 18-gauge perforated-steel angle

Twenty-five ¼-inch- (6-mm-) diameter by 1-inch- (2.5-cm-) long hex bolts and nuts

Sixteen washers to fit hex bolts

Three 3½-inch (9-cm) steel or brass hinges

¾-inch (2-cm) No. 8 wood screws

Screwdriver

Power drill and ¼-inch (6-mm) bit

project tip

063 consider window style

The salvaged window used as the cover will determine the size, shape, and style of your cold frame. The curving lines of the Gothic-inspired window we used made the construction of this cold frame a bit more complicated than building a rectangular structure.

STEP 1 Using a hacksaw, cut wood for sides, each 18 inches (46 cm) tall, matching the window's dimensions while allowing the window to overlap the cold frame by ½ inch (1.25 cm).

STEP 2 Join the side pieces, using 18-gauge perforated-steel angle. Use the ¼-inch (6-mm) hex bolts to attach the angles to the wood, placing a washer between the head of each bolt and the wood.

STEP 3 Attach hinges to the underside of the window frame, using ¾-inch- (2-cm-) long No. 8 wood screws. Lay the window atop the box and use the hinges to mark the location for drilling ¼-inch (6-mm) holes on the outside of the box. Use ¼-inch (6-mm) hex bolts to fasten the hinges to the wood. Place washers between the bolts and wood.

STEP 4 Your cold frame will warm up quickly when the sun is shining directly on it. Always prop open the lid a little on bright sunny days, even if the air temperature is cool. On warm days, you may want to open the lid completely. Always close the lid before nightfall to hold in the day's warmth.

064 compost it!

Composting happens all the time, naturally—think under trees, shrubs, and leaf piles. Setting up a compost bin simply formalizes the process.

MATERIALS

Work gloves

Safety glasses

4 or 5 wooden pallets in similar sizes

1 package 8D galvanized box nails

Hammer

Tape measure

Portable circular saw

Corded or cordless electric drill

3/16-inch (5-mm) drill bit

1 package 2½-inch (6.5-cm) No. 8 exterior screws

Two 6-foot (1.8-m) 1×6 dog-eared cedar fence boards

1 package 1⅝-inch (40-mm) No. 8 exterior screws

No. 2 Phillips screwdriver or driver bit

Angle square or combination square

STEP 1 Wearing work gloves and safety glasses, set out pallets for the back and side panels. Use the "top" (with the most slats) for the back panel. Fill in wide gaps with slats from spare pallets so any remaining gaps are less than 2 inches (5 cm) wide. Attach the slats to the pallet frame with 8D galvanized nails.

STEP 2 Place side and back pallets on edge. Remove any nails and other debris from the pallets' heavy rails; cut to match the width of the finished bin. Drill pilot holes through the rails (A) and set them on the top edges of bin panels, with one rail along the back edge and one at approximately the center mark. Attach the rails to the bin pallets with 2½-inch (6.5-cm) screws (B).

STEP 3 Flip the bin assembly on its back to expose what will be the bottom edges of the panel pallets (C).

STEP 4 From a 1×6 cedar fence plank, cut two diagonal braces for the corners; to measure at least 18 inches (46 cm) point to point, ends miter-cut at 45 degrees. Attach a brace at each corner using 1⅝-inch (4-cm) screws (D).

STEP 5 Cut the other cedar fence plank to length and attach it to the front ends of the two side panels (E).

STEP 6 Attach the center rail along the top (F). These boards will act as ties to keep the bin sides from spreading.

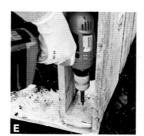

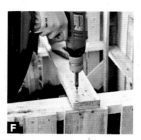

project tip

065 site it right

Designate a spot for composting that's out of sight but not too long a hike from the kitchen. It should measure a minimum of 3 feet (1 m) square. Fill your compost bin with discarded fruits and veggies, tea bags, and plant matter to increase nitrogen, and include egg shells and their compostable cardboard crates to provide minerals that will help with decomposition. Keep two piles—one finished and ready for use in the garden and another for adding new material.

066 round up rainwater

To give your plants natural, untreated water as well as save money on water bills, consider the age-old wisdom of collecting rainwater.

MATERIALS

Drill and ½-inch (13-mm) hole bit

½-inch (1.25-cm) spigot

55-gallon (208-L) plastic barrel with clamp-on lid

Two ⅞-inch (2.25-cm) flat metal washers

1-inch (2.5-cm) OD× ¾-inch (2-cm) ID O-ring (rubber faucet ring)

Plumber's tape

¾×2¼×⅛-inch (2×57×3-cm) rubber washer

½-inch (1.25-cm) lock nut

¾-inch (2-cm) lock nut wrench

Silicone caulk

1×¾-inch (2.5×2-cm) overflow valve

¾-inch (2-cm) lock nut

Downspout diverter with additional extension

Utility knife

STEP 1 Drill a hole for the spigot 1 foot (30 cm) from the barrel's bottom to allow space for a watering can (A). Drill a hole for an overflow valve approximately 2 inches (5 cm) from the top of the barrel.

STEP 2 Assemble the spigot, O-ring, and metal washer on the outside of the barrel (B); on the inside of the barrel, wrap the spigot stem threads with plumber's tape, then add the rubber washer and lock nut. Use a wrench to tighten the assembly. Seal the inside and the outside of the spigot with a bit of silicone caulk.

STEP 3 Assemble the overflow valve, metal washer, and lock nut (C). Seal the valve using silicone caulk on the inside and outside of the barrel.

STEP 4 Using the bottom of the downspout diverter as a guide, cut an opening in the barrel lid with a utility knife. Attach the diverter to the downspout, and guide one end of it into the barrel (D). Add a downspout extension to the other end of the diverter. Set the diverter switch to direct water into the rain barrel or into the extended downspout.

STEP 5 Use the spigot to attach a hose or fill a watering can (D).

A

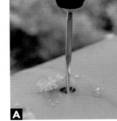

B

C

D

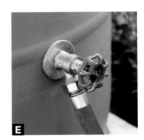

E

project tip

067 winterize your barrel

If you live in a warm climate, you can use your rain barrel all year long. But if you live in a cold climate, you need to take steps to prevent damage—a full barrel can bulge and split with the expansion of frozen water. Drain the barrel and leave the spigot open during freezing weather. It doesn't hurt to remove the hoses, either.

068 create your own nursery

Nurturing new life from seeds, bulbs, and young nursery stock provides a wealth of inexpensive plants for your garden.

ANNUALS (A) For a year of bountiful blooms such as the marigolds shown here, saturate peat pellets with water until they swell into plantable pods. Sow a few seeds in each pod; place in the seed-starting tray and cover the tray with its clear plastic lid. Set the growing tray on a heating pad until the seeds germinate. Set the seedlings in a sunny window for a month or so. When the seedlings have developed two sets of leaves, they are ready for potting. Fill 3-inch (8-cm) peat pots halfway with potting mix, set a pod of seedlings in each pot, and cover the pod with seed-starting mix. Whenever you water the seedlings, include a dose of soluble fertilizer.

PERENNIALS (B) For flowers that return year after year, such as the hardy geranium 'Azure Rush' shown here,

water the young perennial, also known as a plug, with a solution of fertilizer, then plant it in a 4-inch (10-cm) nursery pot. Water before planting. Water plantings regularly when the soil begins to dry. After two months, gently tip the plant out of the nursery pot to check the root growth. When the roots have filled the bottom of the pot, it is time to transplant into a 2- or 3-gallon (7.5- or 11.5-L) nursery pot. Sprinkle a handful of slow-release fertilizer into the potting mix. Water the plant regularly. At summer's end, transplant the well-developed perennial into the garden, where it will establish itself and grow new roots before winter.

SUMMER BULBS (C) To grow bulbs such as the Oriental lily shown here, fill a gallon nursery pot halfway with potting mix. Set three bulbs on the potting mix, with pointed ends up and space between them. Cover the bulbs and fill the pot with potting mix. Water after planting and when the soil begins to dry. When the plants have developed, transplant them into a sunny spot in the garden. Toss a handful of 5-10-10 fertilizer into the planting hole. Your bulbs will bloom within weeks. Fertilize again when the plants flower to encourage their return the next year.

069 pot it up

Get up and growing by setting up a potting area.

MATERIALS

7 lightweight square pavers

Straight-edge garden spade

Trowel

Heavy protective gloves

Paver base

Potting bench

Storage tubs with locking lids

Wire compost bin

STEP 1 Determine the placement of the standing pad and dig out an area large enough to accommodate all the pavers laid side by side without space between them (A). Use the spade and the trowel to remove soil to a depth equal to the thickness of a paver plus 1 inch (2.5 cm).

STEP 2 Wearing gloves, smooth a 1-inch (2.5-cm) layer of paver base over the area, leveling it with your hand (B).

STEP 3 Set pavers in place one at a time (C). When a paver is in place with no gaps between it and surrounding pavers, stand on the paver to press it down into the paver base. Make sure it is level and does not rock from side to side when you step on it. Add or remove paver base as needed. When all pavers are set properly, put the potting bench in place. Add storage bins for tools and potting soil and set up a wire compost bin nearby.

070 raise your veggies

Trimmed with cedar, this raised bed has a sleek look, making the vegetable garden pretty enough for the front yard. Even in winter, the raised bed will provide structure and interest.

MATERIALS

10-foot (3-m) 1×4 cedar board

6-foot (1.8-m) 1×4 cedar board

8-foot (2.5-m) 1×4 cedar board

4-foot (1.2-m) ¼×1 cedar slat

8×2-foot (245×60-cm) sheet of 2-inch (5-cm) corrugated galvanized metal roofing material

Off-set metal snips

Stain

3-inch (8-cm) paintbrush

8 corner brackets

Box of fifty 1-inch (2.5-cm) No. 10 self-piercing hex screws, with neoprene washers

¼-inch (6-mm) magnetic hex screwdriver or drill bit

STEP 1 Before you begin, have the cedar wood cut at your lumber store. Cut the 10-foot (3-m) cedar board in half for the two long top pieces. Cut the 6-foot (1.8-m) cedar board in half for the two short top pieces. Cut the 8-foot- (2.5-m-) long cedar board into eight 1-foot (30-cm) lengths for the leg pieces. Cut the 4-foot- (1.2-m-) long cedar slat into four 1-foot (30-cm) lengths for the inside supports.

STEP 2 Cut the metal in half lengthwise, making two 1×8-foot (30×245-cm) panels (A). Next, cut both panels at the 3-foot (90-cm) mark to form the ends of the raised bed. The remaining two

1×5-foot (30×150-cm) panels will form the sides.

STEP 3 Stain the cut boards (B).

STEP 4 Connect each of the four wooden top horizontal sides with corner brackets (C). Use two screws on each board end to keep it stable. You'll have a 3×5-foot (90×150-cm) frame.

STEP 5 Build the four leg pieces by connecting two 1-foot (30-cm) lengths with corner brackets, using two screws on each board (D). These will support the 3×5-foot (90×150-cm) frame and serve as footings for the raised bed.

STEP 6 Screw in the first metal side (E). Position legs at both ends of the box frame, and lay the metal side in the section. Screw along the inside of the sides and legs to connect these three pieces. Be sure the cut metal edge points toward the ground. Repeat to join all four sides of the raised bed.

STEP 7 Place the raised bed where desired. From the inside, secure each of the four 1-foot (30-cm) slats at the mid point to increase the stability of the metal (F). Once in place, firmly press the legs slightly into the ground; loosening the soil if the ground is hard.

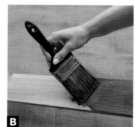

071 make a lampshade cloche

Protect tasty seedlings from squirrels and other nibblers with this clever cover.

MATERIALS

Protective gloves

Wire cutters

Galvanized chicken wire (poultry netting)

Lampshade with the fabric removed

Needle-nose pliers

Spray paint

Decorative knob with nut

Hacksaw

STEP 1 While wearing protective gloves, use wire cutters to cut a section of chicken wire large enough to wrap around the sides of the lampshade frame (A). Cut a smaller piece to fit the top of the lampshade.

STEP 2 Wrap the chicken wire around the frame, snipping off excess. Use the needle-nose pliers to wrap wire ends around the frame (B). Crimp the sharp edges inward.

STEP 3 In a well-ventilated area, paint the cloche (C). Let dry.

STEP 4 Insert the decorative knob into the ring at the top of the lampshade and mark the bolt at the bottom of the ring (D). Use the hacksaw to trim the knob's bolt just beyond the mark, allowing room to screw on the nut.

STEP 5 Attach the knob with the nut that came with it (E), and your cloche is ready for duty in the garden.

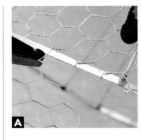

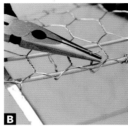

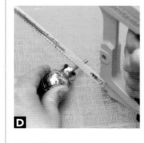

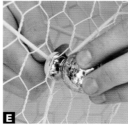

072 step up to ladder shelves

Charming in its own right, a ladder provides geometric form in pleasing contrast to billowing flower-cloaked shrubs and frothy perennials.

MATERIALS

Two stepladders (approximately the same height)

2×2 lumber, cut to the desired lengths (you will need about seven pieces per shelf)

1×2 crosspieces (you will need supports every 18 to 24 inches [46–60 cm], cut to the depth of the shelf)

Drill

Screws

STEP 1 Build the shelves. The shelves of the potting station are easy to make. About 7 feet (2 m) long, each consists of about seven 2×2 lumber pieces spaced about 1 inch (2.5 cm) apart, creating a slatted appearance. (For ample storage and display, make the shelves as wide as your ladders will allow, but here seven 2x2s did the trick.) Secure the slats every 18 to 24 inches (46–60 cm) with a 1×2 crosspiece and screws.

STEP 2 Set up the ladders. Because a strong wind can topple them, site the potting station carefully. A protected area near a building that blocks dominant winds is a good choice. Expand the ladders completely, and situate their bases about 5 feet (1.5 m) apart. Be sure the step sides of the ladders face toward the inside of the potting station.

STEP 3 After setting up the ladders, put the slatted shelves in place. Set them atop the ladder steps to extend through the ladders at least 8 inches (20 cm). Attach the shelves to the ladders with screws. Outfit the new garden work space with tools, pots, bags of soil, plants, and vintage garden items.

project tip

073 paint it pretty

To add a touch of color, paint the lumber before assembling the shelves. A coat of paint or varnish, if you prefer a natural wood look, will protect the shelves from moisture.

074 put together a potting bench

Old pallets hold many possibilities. See how to transform one (or two) into a beautiful and functional potting bench.

MATERIALS

1 or 2 wooden pallets

Framing hammer

Pry bar

Measuring tape

Straightedge

Pencil

Miter saw or circular saw

2×4 lumber (optional)

Table saw

1⅝-inch (40-mm) galvanized exterior screws

Screw gun

Glue (optional)

Level

Drill

Sandpaper

Tack cloth or vacuum

Stain and polyurethane or primer and paint

STEP 1 Disassemble the pallet(s) using a hammer and pry bar (A). Be careful not to damage the ends of the boards. Select the widest, best-looking boards for the countertop. Measure the salvaged wood; its dimensions will determine the width of the finished bench. (A good size is about 40 inches [1 m] wide.)

STEP 2 Using a straightedge, pencil, and miter or circular saw, mark (B) and trim away splintered wood and square the edges of the boards. Cut off knotholes and other weak parts of the boards for a strong potting bench.

STEP 3 Use the pallet base boards or 2×4 lumber for three legs. Break down

a second pallet or join two pallet pieces with screws for a fourth leg. To make the 5-foot (1.5-m) back legs, "sister" two of the 2×4 pieces with additional lumber from the other pallet 2×4 base pieces or 1× lumber cut to the width of the leg pieces. Cut an 8-inch (20-cm) notch in each board and join with screws (C); glue.

STEP 4 Attach a 26-inch (66-cm) 1× board to each back leg (D); this will be the depth of the bench. Screw it perpendicular and to the inside of the leg piece so the top of the board will be 3 feet (90 cm) from the ground. Screw a front leg to the 1× piece to have a configuration resembling a lowercase h. Repeat to have two identical pieces that will serve as the framework for the left and right sides of your bench.

STEP 5 Add one countertop board at the back of the bench to support it, then position the front face board, or skirt, and install it. "Sister" the front legs to match the thickness of the back legs. Flip the bench over and install the back skirt to complete the frame (E).

STEP 6 Measure and install blocks on the back legs in the spaces directly in front of the back skirt (F). You will screw the final countertop piece into these blocks.

STEP 7 Choose your countertop pieces, lay

continued on next page

A

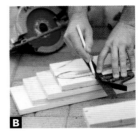
B

C

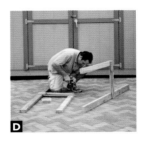
D

E

F

continued from previous page

them flush with each other from front to back, and screw them into place (G). The front countertop piece can overlap the front skirt slightly if you wish. You will have to cut the last piece to the appropriate width and length to fit between the back legs.

STEP 8 To create supports for the bottom shelf, about 7 inches (18 cm) above the ground attach 1× pieces to the front and back legs on each side (H). To ensure consistent shelf height, you can install temporary spacers (the long piece parallel to and touching the ground) and measure the distance between the tops of the spacers and the tops of the shelf-support pieces.

STEP 9 Screw in the bottom shelf pieces using 1× material and in the same manner as for the countertop. Add a 1× board for the top shelf, screwing it into the tops of the back legs. Install more 1× boards to form the back slats (J), generously and evenly spacing the boards so you can hook things over them in the future (I). Use a level to make sure the slats are straight.

STEP 10 Using 1× material, measure for length and cut two back bracing blocks with 45-degree ends. Drill holes into the edges so the blocks won't split when you screw them into place (J). Start screws into the blocks.

STEP 11 Position the bracing blocks on the insides of the back legs and back skirt. Drive screws into the back legs, the countertop, and the back skirt. Drill in the back-skirt screws from the outside (K). These blocks will prevent side-to-side motion of the potting bench.

STEP 12 Remove all rough, splinter-inducing spots with sandpaper (L).

STEP 13 Wipe down or vacuum the bench to remove wood dust. Stain or paint the bench (M). Apply one coat of stain, then two coats of polyurethane, following the label instructions for drying times. If you paint, apply two coats of primer and two coats of paint for a long-lasting finish.

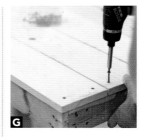

075 prop up flowers with a fence

When flowers want to flop, support them gracefully with a rustic bentwood panel.

MATERIALS

Loppers

Pruning shears

Three 30-inch- (76-cm-) long branches, approximately 1 inch (2.5 cm) in diameter

Three 3-foot- (90-cm-) long branches, less than 1 inch (2.5 cm) in diameter

1½-inch (4-cm) wallboard nails

Hammer

Scrap lumber wedges

Wire cutters

16-gauge tie wire

Pliers

Two 25-inch (64-cm) long branches, about ½ inch (1.25 cm) in diameter

45-inch- (115-cm-) long flexible whip or woody shoot

1-inch (2.5-cm) 17-gauge wire nails

STEP 1 After gathering your branches with garden loppers and pruning shears, lay out your design using the 30-inch (76-cm) long pieces as the upright posts. Set the outside posts about 30 inches (76 cm) apart, and place the center upright slightly higher than the end posts. Lay the three 3-foot (90-cm) crosspieces on top, placing the lowest crosspiece roughly 1 foot (30-cm) above the bottom of the upright posts (A). The crosspieces will extend about 3 inches (8 cm) beyond the posts on either side. The bottom of the center upright should be just slightly below the lowest crosspiece.

STEP 2 Nail the crosspieces to each of the upright posts (B). If necessary, use scrap lumber wedges to support the stems and prevent stems from splitting while driving the nails.

STEP 3 Turn the panel over. Snip pieces of wire long enough to wrap around the joints, and use pliers to twist the wire, making tight joints (C) at every junction between crosspieces and the posts.

STEP 4 Turn the panel face up and position the ray pieces in a V-shape. Use wire nails to secure the rays to the crosspieces where they meet. Bend the long whip and place it on top of everything, nailing it onto the panel in at least three places (D). When you place your flower fence in the garden, dig small holes for the posts with a trowel. Firm the soil around the posts.

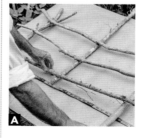
A

B

C

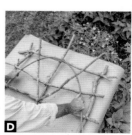
D

076 protect your berries

Keep birds and other creatures from feasting on your berries with an oversize globe cage.

MATERIALS

Three 10-foot (3-m) PEX tubes

Tape measure

Six 20-inch (50-cm) PEX tubes

Six ¾-inch (2-cm) plastic tee connectors

Drill

14×14-foot (4.25×4.25-m) piece of ¾-inch (2-cm) black mesh bird netting

4-inch (10-cm) cable ties

4-inch (10-cm) bolt

⁵⁄₁₆-inch (8-mm) flat metal washer

Wood finial, knob, or garden pick (optional)

STEP 1 Measure and mark the center of each 10-foot (3-m) PEX tube (A).

STEP 2 For the globe cage base, connect the six 20-inch (50-cm) segments of PEX tubing with the tee connectors (B) to form a ring. Fitting the last segments together can be tricky—it's easier with a second person to help. Make sure the center prong of each tee connector points upward (C).

STEP 3 Slip one end of a 10-foot (3-m) tube over an upright tee connector. Carefully bend the tube and slip the other end onto a connector on the opposite side of the base ring, angling the opening of each tee connector outward to arch the tubing. Repeat with the other two 10-foot (3-m) lengths of PEX.

STEP 4 Drill a hole through each center mark (D) on the PEX tubes at the apex of the arch.

STEP 5 Cover the frame tautly with bird netting, attaching to the PEX with cable ties (E). Make sure there are no open gaps for small animals to crawl through. Leave the bottom of the frame open so you can pop the lightweight cage on and off your berry plant to harvest your crop.

STEP 6 Working from inside the cage, insert the bolt through the washer and the three center holes in the PEX. Screw the finial onto the bolt (F) to create a decorative handle.

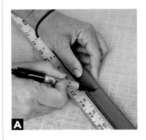
A

B

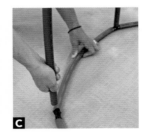
C

D

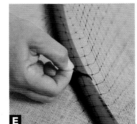
E

F

project tip

077 simplify with string

If you don't want to crown your cage with a wood finial, knob, or garden pick, simply wrap the PEX intersection at the dome's top with colored wire or garden twine to secure the tubes.

078 build a broken-brick patio

Broken bricks are perfect for making a charming crazy-quilt pavement.

MATERIALS

Bricks

Gravel

Sand (ask your building-supply retailer how much gravel and sand you need based on your specific area)

Mason's hammer with striking head and chisel

8×8-inch (20×20-cm) tamper

Dead-blow rubber mallet

Shovel

Broom

STEP 1 Use a mason's hammer to break bricks into smaller pieces or chip old mortar off bricks.

STEP 2 Excavate the area and lay a base of about 1½ inches (4 cm) of gravel. Tamp down the gravel and top with 1½ inches (4 cm) of masonry sand. Establish a brick edge first and then place a couple of odd-shape stones into the design. Begin to fill the space in with brick pieces (A); tamp the bricks into place with a mallet.

STEP 3 Continue, placing the bricks as close together as possible (B). The size and shape of your bricks may suggest fanciful patterns.

STEP 4 After the bricks are in place, use a shovel to spread sand over the area (C).

STEP 5 Sweep the sand between the bricks with a broom (D). You might need to add more sand and sweep the area a couple of times to fill in all the gaps.

079 grow up!

Send pole beans scrambling up homemade tepees for easy bean harvesting and striking vertical presence. Pole beans produce two to three times more beans than bush beans in the same space.

STEP 1 Construct a tepee or other trellis to support pole beans before seeding to avoid damaging plant roots later. Lash three 8- to 10-foot- (2.5 to 3-m-) long bamboo stakes together with garden twine to form a tepee (A) and create a season-long support for the vigorous pole beans. Sink the stakes at least 1 foot (30 cm) into the ground.

STEP 2 After the chance of frost has passed, plant bean seeds directly into loose garden soil (B).

STEP 3 Harvest beans when the pod is full, crisp, and fully elongated (C) but before the seed within the pod is fully developed. For weeks-long harvest, pick beans every couple of days.

080 raise your cukes

Handsome plants and a generous harvest make cucumbers ideal for this helpful vining tower.

MATERIALS

Four 8-foot (2.5-m) 1×2 pine furring strips

Saw

Cordless drill

1¼-inch (3-cm) No. 8 screws

One quart exterior latex paint

2-inch (5-cm) paintbrush

18- to 20-inch- (46–50-cm-) diameter container with drainage hole

Potting soil

Cucumber seeds

STEP 1 For a 4-foot (1.2-m) tall cucumber tower, cut two furring strips in half for the uprights. To make a tower 10 inches (25 cm) wide, cut sixteen 9½-inch (24-cm) crosspieces and a 10½-inch (27-cm) long spacer (A).

STEP 2 Construct each face of the tower separately. Attach the crosspieces to the uprights, driving the 1¼-inch (3-cm) No. 8 screws through the wider sides (B). One screw for each joint is sufficient. Start at the top, and use the spacer to measure down between crosspieces, attaching four crosspieces on each upright. The tower legs (which will be inserted into the soil) will be about 11 inches (28 cm) long.

STEP 3 Put the panels together (one upright in each corner) by attaching the free ends of one set of crosspieces to the already fastened joints on another (C). Start the screws into the crosspieces, not into the uprights. Do one set of corners at a time, working your way around.

STEP 4 Paint the tower with two coats of exterior latex paint; let dry (D). Fill the container with potting soil, set the tower in the pot, pushing the legs into the soil, and plant five or six cucumber seeds. The seeds should be close to the tower legs, not the edge of the pot. Water well. The seeds germinate quickly (within a week). After they have sprouted and start to grow, thin to no more than three plants. Cucumbers have tendrils to grasp the trellis, but you'll also need to gently direct the vines up into the structure while they are young and supple to keep them from sprawling.

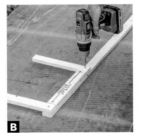

081 choose a vining variety

Cukes aren't the only edible option for filling your tower. Other vining plants, such as berries, beans, squash, grapes, or edible flowers will vine up the structure for a nice full harvest as well.

082 hop to it!

Hop vines clamber over a metal arbor to evoke the industrial style of a microbrewery.

MATERIALS

Bolt cutter

Four 3½×7-foot (1×2-m) sheets of steel remesh

Six 10-foot (3-m) lengths of rebar

Hacksaw

6-inch (15-cm) nylon cable ties

16-gauge wire

½-inch (1.25-cm) metal pipe straps

Screw eyes

Two large planters (we used cedar trough-style planters)

Three 7-foot (2-m) lengths of rebar

Potting soil

Two hop rhizomes (we used *Humulus lupulus* 'Cascade' and 'Chinook')

STEP 1 Use a bolt cutter to trim the remesh sheets into two 2×7-foot (60×215-cm) sections, two 2×2-foot (60×60-cm) sections, and one 2×6-foot (60×180-cm) panel (A).

STEP 2 For each arbor side, lay a 2×7-foot (60×215-cm) and a 2×2-foot (60×60-cm) section of remesh on the ground to form a 2×9-foot (60×275-cm) panel. Top with three 10-foot (3-m) rods of rebar, placing a rod on each outer long edge and one in the center. The rods can extend longer than the panels or be trimmed to eliminate overhang (we left ours longer). Attach remesh to the rebar with cable ties at each intersection (B). Hide the plastic cable ties by wrapping with wire.

STEP 3 If using wood containers, attach one assembled side panel to the outer side of each planter with metal pipe straps, two per rebar (C). Set the planters, with arbor side panels on the outer sides, in place on either side of the entrance.

STEP 4 For the arbor top, place the three 7-foot (2-m) rebars horizontally on top of the remesh side panels. Secure the horizontal rebar rods to the vertical rebars with cable ties, adjusting to make the top level (D). Set the final 2×6-foot (60×180-cm) remesh section over the horizontal rebars and secure with cable ties to finish the top panel.

STEP 5 Fill planters with well-draining potting soil. Plant a hop rhizome horizontally in each planter about 1 inch (2.5 cm) below the soil surface (E).

A

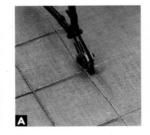
B

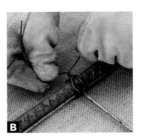

C

D

E

project tip

083 keep hops covered

Mulch to help retain moisture. Hop plants concentrate on developing root systems during the first growing season. Full growth generally occurs the second year.

084 build an arbor

A kit enables you to make a stylish arbor in a weekend that will enhance your garden for years.

MATERIALS

Arbor kit

Exterior stain or
 polyurethane

Paintbrush

Wood screws

Carpenter's square

Tape measure

Power drill

Four 2-foot (60-cm)
 lengths of rebar

Concrete mix

STEP 1 Apply exterior stain or polyurethane to the arbor pieces and allow the finish to dry for 24 hours before assembly. Lay out the arbor parts on a clean, flat surface, such as a driveway or yard.

STEP 2 Line up the pilot holes and attach the side panels to the header board using wood screws (A). Use a carpenter's square and tape measure to ensure the structure is square as you proceed. Turn the assembly over to repeat the process and attach the other header board.

STEP 3 Attach the cap pieces to the header, using a spacer as a guide (B). Screw each cap board into place consecutively. Stand the arbor up to see if it's wobbly. Tighten screws if needed.

STEP 4 Anchor the arbor to its site, using 2-foot-(60-cm-) long rebar. Slide rebar into the groove of each leg (C). Set the rebar anchors in concrete to secure the arbor and prevent it from tipping.

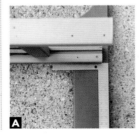
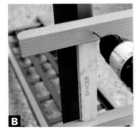

085 take a garden to new heights

Small but mighty, raised-bed gardens overflow with produce and make homegrown goodies a possibility nearly anywhere.

Gardening in a box is a little like opening a gift filled with infinite treasures. Just when you think you've found the last present in the depths of the box, you stumble upon yet another jewel. Garden boxes, or raised beds, are rife with tasty homegrown gifts from spring until a hard frost. From crisp greens and radishes in April to pounds of tomatoes and peppers in July to broccoli and spinach in October, well-planned garden boxes produce edible gifts for months while occupying just a 3 to 4 feet (1–1.2 m) of space.

The small footprint is just one benefit of gardening in raised beds. These garden workhorses boast so many additional advantages that growers who have long turned soil in traditional in-ground beds are moving to raised beds.

EXTEND THE SEASON One of the chief advantages of garden boxes is early-season planting. Air moves around the 12- to 18-inch- (30–46-cm-) tall beds in early spring, drying and warming the soil and making it fit for planting as much as two weeks earlier than in-ground gardens. Early planting dates benefit from cool spring growing conditions to produce lush heads of broccoli and rows of tender baby greens long before the heat of summer sets in.

Elevated crops are also a convenient way to extend the garden season in autumn. Any frost protection or extra watering needed at the end of the season is made easy in the compact planting area.

REDUCE WORK Raised beds simply make gardening easier. A moderate 1-foot (30-cm) elevation of the planting surface might not sound like much of an advantage, but bending, stooping, and reaching to care for plants becomes vastly easier with this small lift.

DETER CRITTERS Raised beds are also excellent solutions for challenging garden issues. A layer of chicken wire placed at the bottom of the box can thwart moles, while a cover of netting will deter birds. As another bonus, intensive planting, combined with mulching, eliminates most weeding chores.

IMPROVE SOIL One of the greatest benefits of raised beds is that they make way for healthy, well-drained soil. Even if the ground below your compost-rich soil is mostly clay or sand, you'll be able to grow a bountiful crop of flavor-rich produce just outside your door.

four ways to flavor your garden

Planting a garden around a particular theme—an ethnic cuisine or salad garden, for instance—is a fun way to ensure you always have the freshest ingredients on hand for your favorite foods.

086 cook italian

A garden themed around Italian cooking of course includes a good sauce tomato such as tomato 'Amish Paste' (A). Other vital ingredients in this Italian kitchen garden include garlic (F), thyme (B), rosemary (C), Italian basil (J), Italian parsley (E), pepper 'Sweet California Wonder' (D), and carrot 'Bolero' (G). Bite-size Roma grape tomato 'Juliet' (H) is perfect for snacking and salads—and no Italian garden is complete without some dark leafy greens, such as kale (I), for sautéeing or stewing.

087 toss a salad

Salad greens taste freshest and have the highest nutrient content right after they are picked. With a salad garden, you can snip tender baby greens minutes before you eat them. A good mix includes kale 'Darkibor' (A), lettuce 'Flashy Trout Back' (B), Swiss chard 'Bright Lights' (C), pak choy (D), spinach 'Catalina' (E), and lettuce 'Sweetie Baby Romaine' (F). Toss with a vinaigrette of 1 part vinegar to 3 parts olive oil, a little Dijon mustard, and some salt and fresh-ground pepper and you are good to go!

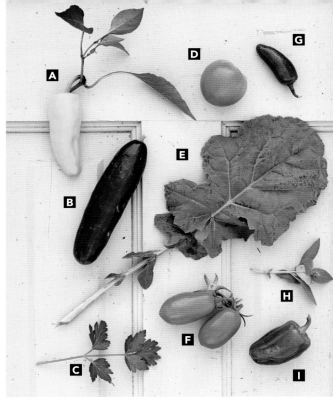

088 season it with herbs

The bright flavor of fresh herbs brings foods alive. Planting an herb garden means you can pick just what you need. There's no waste, as there often is when you buy fresh herbs at the store. A good basic herb garden includes the following: sage (A), dill (B), thyme (C), cilantro (D), Italian basil (E), chives (F), variegated sage (G), Italian parsley (H), Thai basil (I), rosemary (J), oregano (K), and lavender (L).

089 go to market

While the purpose of an actual market garden is to grow vegetables to sell at a farmer's market, you can create your own market garden with a few things you use most commonly in your kitchen. For most people, this is a few tomatoes, peppers, cucumbers, an herb or two, and a dark leafy green. Our market garden includes pepper 'Gypsy' (A), cucumber 'Bush Champion' (B), Italian parsley (C), tomato 'Patio Princess' (D), kale (E), tomato 'Little Mama' (F), jalapeño pepper (G), basil (H), and pepper 'California Sweet Wonder' (I).

090 twist an arbor

Small branches unite around a simple rebar frame to form a charming country-style arbor.

MATERIALS

Two 10-foot (3-m) lengths of ½-inch (1.25-cm) rebar

Pipe wrench

1 foot (30 cm) any type of small-gauge wire

Wire cutters

Small branches in various sizes

Pruners

6-inch (15-cm) nylon cable ties

STEP 1 Select the spot for your arch. Working on one side of the location, use your hands to push one piece of rebar into the ground as far as possible. Screw the pipe wrench onto the rebar and use your body weight to sink the rebar to about 1 foot (30 cm) in the ground (A). Repeat the process on the other side with the second rebar.

STEP 2 Beginning about 7 feet (2 m) above ground level, use the pipe wrench to slowly bend one rebar to form an arch (B). Repeat with the second rebar. The two bent pieces of rebar will overlap at the top of the arch.

STEP 3 Wire the two rebars together at the top of the arch, forming a frame for the twig arbor (C).

STEP 4 Small branches of various sizes are useful in creating an eye-pleasing arch. Aim to collect and prepare at least 60 sticks to begin constructing the arbor; collect more twigs to add them to the structure later if needed. Prepare branches by pruning off small side twigs (D).

STEP 5 Working with two or three twigs at a time, place them against the structure and tie to the rebar with a cable tie (E). Continue adding sticks, placing those that naturally bend to form an arch near the top of the structure. Secure them with cable ties. Soon the rebar structure will be hidden and you can secure new stick bundles to twigs that are already attached to the rebar. Finish by trimming the cable tie tails and pruning wayward twigs.

A

B

C

D

E

091 add color to your arch

To give your quirky arch a splash of color, plant blooming vines at the base and let them climb: Black-eyed Susan vine, Cardinal climber vine, Moonflower vine, Morning glory 'Grandpa Otts,' and Sweet pea varieties will all climb up nicely.

092 have a seat

A little effort and a few hardworking materials result in a sturdy yet stunning bench well suited for the organic shapes of the garden.

MATERIALS

Three 5-foot (1.5-m) cedar 4×4s

Two 5-foot (1.5-m) cedar 2×4s

Four 1-foot (30-cm) cedar 2×2s

Circular saw

Sandpaper

Sixteen 7×10½-inch (18×27-cm) paver stones

Drill

3-inch (8-cm) deck screws

Teak oil finish

Shovel

Pea gravel (about 2 bags)

Level

Two tubes landscape adhesive

STEP 1 Cut the 4×4s and 2×4s so the ends line up. Angle the ends of the 2×2s if desired. Sand the ends and top.

STEP 2 Arrange the 4×4s and 2×4s in an alternating pattern with ½ inch (1.25 cm) space between them (A). (Try using a ½-inch- [1.25-cm-] wide scrap of wood as a spacer.) To create a temporary bracket for the base, set two pavers on the bottom of the bench, 10 inches (25 cm) from each edge, and place the 2×2s on either side of a paver. Remove the pavers and secure the 2×2s with deck screws (B). Apply teak oil to protect wood surfaces and let dry.

STEP 3 Using the bracketed spaces on the bottom of the bench as a guide, dig two holes about 21 inches (53 cm) apart. The holes should be 4 inches (10 cm) deep and slightly larger than a paver (C).

STEP 4 Fill each hole with 3 inches (8 cm) of pea gravel and tamp down firmly.

STEP 5 Place a paver on top of the gravel and level it to ground height (D). Repeat with the second side, checking to make sure they are both level (E).

STEP 6 Stack pavers, using adhesive between layers (F) until you have eight on each side. Set the bench seat on the bases, fitting the brackets snugly on either side of the top paver. Secure the seat to the bases with landscaping adhesive.

093 get lumber pre-cut

If you buy lumber at a large home improvement center, a staff person can cut the wood to the size you need.

094 put a hole in your wall

A pattern of circles suggesting effervescent bubbles is a simple way to dress up a plain wooden fence or gate. The result is more ventilation and peekaboo openings.

MATERIALS

Pattern or stencil

Ruler

Pencil

Wooden fence or gate

Drill with hole-making attachments (we used 4-, 3-, and 2-inch [10-, 8-, and 5-cm] hole saw drill attachments to create our pattern)

Screwdriver

Stain/sealant

Paintbrush

STEP 1 Even a series of apparently random circles will benefit from a pattern, so create a stencil or template to plan your design (A).

STEP 2 Using a ruler as a guide, draw a vertical line on the fence every 1 foot (30 cm) to make a grid to keep your pattern straight (B).

STEP 3 If not using a stencil to draw circles on your fence, trace around the hole saw (C). Refer to the pattern, using it as a guide for where to place the circles within the grid. Two or three different sizes will make the pattern more interesting.

STEP 4 Drill holes according to your pattern (D). An auxiliary handle attached to the drill will help your control. An electric drill will have more power for tackling the project than a cordless version.

STEP 5 Use a screwdriver to pop plugs of wood out of the hole saw (E).

STEP 6 Stain the fence (F). We used a blue semitransparent stain to protect the wood and infuse it with color without obscuring the wood grain.

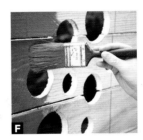

project tip

095 get a helping hand

When you're drilling, it helps to have a second person stand on the opposite side of the fence to push the wood toward you, creating leverage against the pressure of the drill. Be sure your helper is wearing safety gloves and that they set their hands on the areas surrounding your cut, not on top of the drill hole saw.

096 warm up around a flagstone fire pit

Surrounded by native limestone, a classy fire pit is at home in any landscape.

MATERIALS

Shovel or spade

Steel fire pit liner

Flagstone

Pea gravel

STEP 1 Use a sharp shovel to skim the sod off a square area the diameter of the fire pit liner plus 4 feet (1.2 m). For example, if the fire pit liner is 3 feet (90 cm) wide, remove the sod from a 7×7-foot (2×2-m) square. Center the liner in the cleared area and use a shovel or spade to outline the edge of the liner (A). This outline will serve as the excavation guide for the fire pit.

STEP 2 Dig out the soil inside the outline to the depth of the liner (B). The lip of the liner will rest on the ground at grade level.

STEP 3 Place the fire pit liner in the excavated cavity, removing or adding soil as necessary so it is level with the surrounding grade (C).

STEP 4 Place flagstone around the liner to create a fire ring (D). Fitting the irregular limestone slabs is a little like putting together a puzzle. Flip, turn, and rearrange the pieces as necessary until they fit together in an eye-pleasing manner. Aim for a gap of less than 1 inch (2.5 cm) between stones. Fill the gaps with pea gravel to prevent weed growth and to create a finished look. Fill the bottom of the fire pit with a 3-inch (8-cm) layer of pea gravel.

097 build a window well garden

The perfect size for hosting a petite vegetable garden, this 2×3-foot (60×90-cm) raised bed is made using corrugated window wells.

MATERIALS

Two 1-foot- (30-cm-) tall window wells

Two 2-foot (60-cm) 4×4 untreated cedar posts

Twelve 1½-inch (4-cm) lag screws

Screwdriver

Shovel

Topsoil, compost, or quality potting soil

Assorted plants

STEP 1 Position one side of a window well near the top of a 4×4 post. Attach the window well to the post with lag screws (A). Repeat on the other side of the window well. Attach the second window well to the opposite side of the 4×4 posts, forming the raised bed.

STEP 2 Dig two post holes and position the raised bed. Burying the posts anchors the bed, preventing it from shifting during freeze and thaw cycles (B). The bottom of the window well should be flush with the ground.

STEP 3 Fill the garden bed with high-quality topsoil or a mixture of topsoil and compost (C). Quality potting soil is also a good choice. Add soil to within 2 inches (5 cm) of the top of the raised bed.

STEP 4 Maximize planting space by choosing dwarf or bush vegetable plants (D). Patio-size tomato cultivars and bush-type cucumbers are reliable choices. Include herbs for a burst of easy-care flavor all summer.

inviting wildlife

098 plant an avian haven

Turn your garden into a habitat for winged friends with plants, bushes, and trees that provide food and shelter. You'll nourish and appreciate the diversity of nature.

AMERICAN CRANBERRY BUSH (A) Among a diverse group of shrubs that produce bird-friendly berries and offer shelter, this 8- to 15-foot (2.5–4.5-m) variety grows easily and durably.

CRANBERRY COTONEASTER (B) This low, arching, and mounding shrub boasts glossy leaves and red fruits. It's good for slope, terrace, or foundation planting.

STAGHORN SUMAC (C) The fast-growing shrub withstands poor, dry soil. Pollinators feast on its nectar and pollen, and birds feed on the berries.

AMERICAN ELDERBERRY (D) This native shrub reaches 4 to 12 feet (1.2–3.7 m) tall and produces pollen-rich flowers; many birds favor its black berries.

FIRETHORN (E) The dense, thorny branches of this semievergreen to evergreen shrub provide shelter and nesting places as well as berries.

CRABAPPLE (F) The ornamental value of the spring blooms is revered among gardeners; the fruits are the luscious apples of birds' eyes.

ROSE (G) Rose hips—the fruit of roses—vary in size and color, but all prove delectable to birds and other wildlife.

BURNING BUSH (H) This vigorous shrub grows up to 8 feet (2.5 m) tall and provides shelter and nesting sites as well as fruit and seeds.

SERVICEBERRY (I) One of the top plants for birds, this native tree offers nectar-rich spring flowers and sweet summer fruit. (The bird below [I] is a Cedar Waxwing and opposite is a Brown Thrasher.)

HOLLY (J) The brilliant red berries attract Cedar Waxwings and a multitude of other birds throughout winter to this evergreen shrub.

099 make way for monarchs

Turn your garden into a certified monarch magnet—while attract other butterflies—by providing nectar, shelter, and food for caterpillars.

MATERIALS

- 10-inch- (25-cm-) diameter glazed planter saucer
- Plastic flowerpot with 8-inch- (20-cm-) diameter base
- Scissors
- Hammer and nail
- Decorative chain
- Needle-nose pliers
- S hook
- 7-foot- (2-m-) tall shepherd hook garden stake
- Honey
- Water
- Sponges and plastic dish scrubber
- Monarch Waystation sign (if certified)
- 2×2 board
- Spray paint
- Galvanized wire (we used 19-gauge wire)

STEP 1 Measure the plant saucer (the bottom of ours is 8 inches [20 cm] in diameter), and cut a circle that size from the bottom of the plastic flowerpot (A).

STEP 2 Using the hammer and nail, make four holes around the edge of the plastic circle (B).

STEP 3 Create two equal-size lengths of decorative chain, using needle-nose pliers to open links as necessary. (We made two 5-foot [1.5-m] lengths from a 10-foot [3-m] chain.) Open the last link at each end on both chain lengths. Hook each open link to a hole in the plastic circle. Crimp the links closed with the pliers (C). Thread the S hook through a top link in each chain, and hang the S hook from the shepherd hook in your garden. Place the plant saucer on the plastic circle.

STEP 4 Make honey nectar for butterflies by combining 1 part honey and 4 parts water. (We used 1 tablespoon honey and 4 tablespoons water.) Place the sponges and plastic dish scrubber in the saucer. (We cut our sponges into 2½-inch- [6.5-cm-] diameter circles.) Spoon the honey onto the sponges and the dish scrubber.

STEP 5 Go to monarchwatch.org to apply for the certification for your new monarch waystation. The Monarch Watch organization will send you a sign. To mount it in your butterfly refuge, spray-paint a 2×2 board a bright color and attach your Monarch Waystation sign with wire (E). Drive the post into the soil among your most colorful butterfly-attracting flowers.

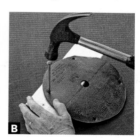
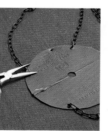

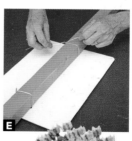

100 plant milkweed

Milkweed is the only food of monarch caterpillars and the only place the butterflies can lay eggs. Plant milkweed to help increase the numbers of migrating monarchs.

101 play water music

The sound of gently trickling water attracts birds to fly in for drinks and splashy baths. This lotuslike dripper attached to a submersible pump enhances a birdbath and creates a delightful garden accent. To make this birdbath, use a 6×48-inch (15×120-cm) PVC pipe as a base, anchoring 1 foot (30 cm) of it into the ground. Wrap the base with a length of twig fencing cut to fit. Set a 3-inch- (8-cm-) deep saucer on the base. Place a few stones in the basin to secure the dripper and provide firm footing for birds. Keep the pump covered with water and behold your feathered friends.

102 grow food for the flock

These plants are more than just beauty queens—they offer a feast for the eyes and food for the birds.

BLACK-EYED SUSAN Yellow flowers bloom all summer and develop black seed heads that are eaten by Oregon Juncos, bushtits, and finches.

BLAZING STAR The spiky flowers of this North American native bloom from the top down. When the red-purple flowers are finished, fuzzy seed heads are left for the birds (pictured at right).

SEDUM 'AUTUMN JOY' Butterflies flock to the pink blooms in fall. The brown, broccoli-shape flower heads remain elegant in winter, providing habitat for insects, which then feed the birds.

CROCOSMIA This flower is a South African native. The 2- to 3-foot- (60–90-cm-) tall hybrid 'Lucifer' has fiery red blooms in summer that draw hummingbirds. The sprays of winter seeds look like beads.

PENCIL CEDAR Aromatic berries offer winter food for birds, such as Cedar Waxwing, as well as cover.

***MAHONIA JAPONICA* 'BEALEI'** Spikes of lemon-yellow flowers on this fall- and winter-blooming *Mahonia* provide much-needed nectar for the Anna's Hummingbird, which winters in the Puget Sound region of Washington State.

PACIFIC WAX MYRTLE This shrub offers birds evergreen cover as well as food from clusters of blackberries favored by the Northern Mockingbird, Northern

Flicker, Red-Bellied Woodpecker, and Wood Thrush.

FILBERT A cross between two species, *C. avellana* and *C. maxima*, 'DuChilly' will cross-pollinate the beaked filbert. A good crop of

these hazelnuts brings both squirrels and Stellar's Jays to get their share of the harvest.

WINTER HEATH Winter-blooming heathers provide nectar for bees that emerge on days warmer than 50°F (10°C).

103 welcome birds home

Encourage winged friends to take up residence in your birdhouses by following these guidelines.

RESEARCH Learn about the nesting habits of birds in your area.

PICK THE RIGHT HOUSE Choose durable, weatherproof birdhouses that have ventilation, drainage holes, and enough depth to accommodate a nest.

START IN FALL Set out birdhouses in fall or early winter if possible.

SITE IT RIGHT Situate a house where birds can find the privacy they need to nest, hatch, and raise broods. Turn the entrance away from high-traffic areas of the yard.

PICK A SUNNY SPOT Select a site in a sunny location shielded from prevailing winds. Place the house close to trees or shrubs.

ROUGH IT UP A rough surface below the entrance hole, inside and outside, helps birds come and go.

PERCH OR NOT? Decide whether a perch outside the entrance is preferable. Some experts say perches are fine; others believe predators use them.

HOST YEAR-ROUND Leave birdhouses up year-round if you prefer. Some cavity-nesting species will use it for shelter in the winter.

CLEAN HOUSE Remove old nesting materials at the beginning of autumn when you are certain breeding season is done.

WASH UP Scrub inside birdhouses using a mild solution of all-natural soap. Set them in the sun to dry thoroughly.

104 make a sparkling basin

The best birdbaths have a rough surface (stone or concrete) and a gradual slope to allow birds sure footing as they wade. For this basin, excavate a bowl shape in soil and line with sand. Mold quick-setting concrete to this shape, and press recycled glass bits in the surface before it begins to set (about 10 minutes). Spritz with water and cover with sheet plastic for three to seven days to cure.

105 provide affordable housing

Nesting or roosting pockets provide cozy shelters for birds, especially in winter and spring.

Put out the welcome mat for your feathered friends by hanging nesting pockets in protected places—among branches of a hedge, large shrub, or vine. Watch for small birds, such as wrens, finches, and chickadees, to move in and keep warm overnight or raise their young in the pouch. Crafted from organic materials such as twigs and grasses, nesting pockets will eventually need replacing.

quick garden tip

106 provide parts and materials

Fill a suet cage with bits of fiber, wood shavings, dog hair, and moss, then hang it in a tree or other place to attract birds. Notice as they begin nesting in spring. Birds expend tremendous energy collecting and weaving bits of dried grasses, stems, leaves, and other garden debris into egg cradles. Help them by offering nest materials, snipped to 6 inches (15 cm) or less, especially if the garden was tidied in fall.

107 serve a birdy buffet

Attract a variety of birds with a bounty-filled standing planter, window box, or hanging basket. In fall or late spring, line a large container with moss and evergreen boughs. Then tuck in fruity branches and seed heads, such as rose hips, red and blue viburnum, golden millet, coneflower, canary grass, broomcorn, and cattail. Top off the display with a small tree-form holly, a weather-worthy birdhouse, and a dish of black sunflower and safflower seeds.

108 make a grapevine birdbath

Suspend an ordinary grapevine wreath from a strong branch for an easy-access wading pool. Tuck twigs in the purchased wreath to enhance its natural look. Use three loops of copper wire to hang the wreath, linking them to a large S hook. Fit a shallow copper dish into your wreath and fill with water.

109 build a bait-box birdhouse

Create a cozy place to nest using cast-off materials that come together in something entirely new.

MATERIALS

Drill equipped with a 1¼-inch (3-cm) hole saw

Vintage bait box (keep an eye out at flea markets or antique stores—a vintage lunch box would work too)

Metal file

Super Glue

Small doorknob plate (or any circular element, such as an old metal button or washer)

Wire cutter

Three vintage house numbers

Epoxy adhesive

4 to 5 feet (1.2–1.5 m) rope

1-inch- (2.5-cm-) wide spring

STEP 1 Using a drill equipped with a 1¼-inch (3-cm) hole saw, drill an entrance hole into the door of the bait box. Smooth the edges of the hole with a metal file.

STEP 2 Apply Super Glue to the back of the doorknob plate and position it about 1 inch (2.5 cm) below the bait box door.

STEP 3 Using a wire cutter, clip the metal points off the backs of the vintage house numbers. (You can use new numbers, if vintage ones prove hard to find.) Apply epoxy adhesive to the backs of the house numbers and position them below the bait box door.

STEP 4 Select the location for your birdhouse. Then measure and cut the desired length of rope to suspend the house. Thread the rope through the top of the bait box and tie it into a knot about 6 inches (15 cm) above the box. Slip the vintage spring onto the rope. Hang your birdhouse.

110 turn a barrel top into a bird bath

An old stump and a galvanized barrel top unite to form a watering hole.

MATERIALS

Chain saw

Stump with the bark removed (ours is about 3 feet [1 m] tall and 2 feet [60 cm] in diameter)

4-inch- (10-cm-) wide metal flashing

Tin snips

Tape measure

Drill

Twenty 2-inch (5-cm) wood screws

Twenty 1-inch (2.5 cm) washers

Twenty ¼-inch (6-mm) washers with ruffled edges

Galvanized barrel top wider than the diameter of the stump

8-inch (20-cm) wood screw

Silicone

Four ½-inch (1.25-cm) wood screws

Two metal handles

STEP 1 Using a chain saw, cut the stump to the desired height, leveling both ends.

STEP 2 Wrap flashing around the bottom of the stump. With tin snips, cut the flashing (leave some overlap). Repeat for the top.

STEP 3 Using a tape measure, mark the top and bottom flashing in equal increments to ensure equal placement of screws and washers.

STEP 4 Use a drill to sink the 2-inch (5-cm) wood screws, each outfitted with a 1-inch (2.5-cm) washer topped with a ¼-inch (6-mm) ruffled washer, into the flashing and the bottom of the stump at the marks you've made. Repeat for the top of the stump.

STEP 5 Drill a hole through the center of the galvanized barrel top. Center the barrel top on the stump. Attach the barrel top to the stump with the 8-inch (20-cm) wood screw.

STEP 6 Apply silicone to seal the area around the screw.

STEP 7 Use the ½ inch (1.25-cm) wood screws and a drill to attach the handles to the stump where desired.

111 encourage good neighbors

If your garden is less than 1 acre (0.4 ha), put up only one birdhouse if you want to attract a particular species. However, Purple Martins, sparrows, and swallows are not territorial and will reside in a community of housing.

112 stack up a birdbath

Make a small birdbath in minutes by stacking a large earthenware saucer on a clay chimney flue liner. Flue liners are inexpensive and can be found at chimney suppliers or repair shops. When you're shopping for saucers (we used a glazed, 18-inch- [46-cm-] diameter saucer), keep in mind that while unglazed terra-cotta basins create a unified look with the chimney liner, those saucers are harder to clean.

113 make a splash with a tomato cage

Turn two utilitarian garden items into a flowery watering spot for birds.

MATERIALS

2 pots black-eyed Susan vine (*Thunbergia alata*)

Trowel

Heavy-duty tomato cage

Plastic pot saucer (make sure it fits neatly into the top of your cage)

STEP 1 In a sunny spot, loosen the soil in an area approximately 18 inches (46 cm) in diameter. Plant the vines near the center of the prepared spot (A).

STEP 2 Place the tomato cage over the vines, pushing it into the soil all the way to the bottom rung of the cage (B). Take care to keep the cage level and straight.

STEP 3 If the vines are long, gently wrap their growing ends on the nearest rungs of the cage; this will encourage them to cover the cage quickly (C).

STEP 4 Place the saucer on top of the cage and fill it with 1 to 2 inches (2.5–5 cm) of water (D). If the cage tips or appears unbalanced, remove the saucer and anchor the cage deeper and straighter before refilling again with water.

STEP 5 Water the vines thoroughly (E).

114 build a barrel-hoop bird feeder

With a little vision and a few nuts and bolts, the treasures at a great junk sale can be transformed into a rustic, country-style bird feeder.

MATERIALS

2-foot- (60-cm-) diameter barrel hoop

Marker

Drill and ¾-inch (20-mm) metal drill bit

Four ¾-inch- (2-cm-) long, 1½-inch- (4-cm-) diameter washers

Six ¾-inch (2-cm) nuts

3-foot- (1-m-) long, ¾-inch- (2-cm-) diameter threaded rod

Two ¾-inch- (2-cm-) long, 2-inch- (5-cm-) diameter washers

18-inch- (46-cm-) diameter cultivator disc

Two ¾-inch (2-cm) couplers

Two 2-inch- (5-cm-) long, ¾-inch- (2-cm-) diameter threaded eye hooks

4-inch (10-cm) spring

Medium-weight rope

STEP 1 Measure the hoop circumference, mark the location for a hole, then mark another hole location on the opposite side of the hoop. Using a ¾-inch (2-cm) drill bit; drill holes at marks (A).

STEP 2 Thread a small washer and a nut onto the rod about 10 inches (25 cm) from one end. Insert the rod through the hole at the hoop top. Tighten with another small washer and a nut on the inside (B).

STEP 3 Place one nut and one large washer on the rod, then insert the rod through the center of the cultivator disc (C).

STEP 4 Place the disc in the hoop center, the large washer flush against the top. Tighten the nut. With a large washer on the rod bottom, tighten a nut on the rod (D).

STEP 5 Place a small washer and nut on the rod. Stretch the hoop; insert the rod in the second hole. Tighten the washer and nut (E).

STEP 6 Place a small washer and a nut on the bottom of the rod; tighten them against the barrel hoop. Thread a coupler onto the bottom of the rod (F).

STEP 7 Thread a coupler onto the top of the rod. Screw an eye hook into the end of each coupler (G).

STEP 8 Add the spring to the eye hook at the top of the feeder. Hang the feeder by securing rope to the top of the spring (H).

STEP 9 Fill the bird feeder with a variety of birdseed to attract different types of flying landscape visitors (I).

115 open a good-bug hotel

Just as birdhouses attract nesting birds, a boutique bug house provides an irresistible shelter for bugs that are beneficial to the garden.

MATERIALS

Two 1-foot (30-cm) 1×6 cedar boards

Two 11-inch (28-cm) 1×6 cedar boards

6-inch (15-cm) 1×6 cedar board

Three 13-inch (33-cm) 1×6 cedar boards

Handsaw

1¼-inch (3-cm) No. 8 screws

Cordless drill and drill bit

2-foot- (60-cm-) wide, ¼-inch- (6-mm-) mesh hardware cloth

Stapler

12-foot (3.7-m) strip of ¼×¾-inch (6×20-mm) screen molding

Hacksaw

Wire nails

Hammer

Natural materials

Moss or straw

Post

STEP 1 Screw the bug house together; our plan creates an asymmetrical house. A 1-foot (30-cm) board will be the base. Attach an 11-inch (28-cm) board perpendicular to one end of the base with two screws up through the bottom. On the other end, attach a 1-foot (30-cm) board. Screw the 6-inch (15-cm) piece to the 13-inch (33-cm) board at a right angle, about 9 inches (23 cm) from the bottom, and then screw the 13-inch (33-cm) center board to the base. Now make the roof: One side is 11 inches (28 cm) long, the other is 13 inches (33 cm) long. Screw them together with a simple butt joint, then screw the roof down onto all three uprights (A).

STEP 2 Cut two 12×16-inch (30×40-cm) pieces of hardware cloth. Staple one hardware cloth panel in place over the back of the structure, then trim any overhang (B).

STEP 3 Cover the sharp ends of the hardware cloth with thin strips of screen molding. Secure each piece of trim with two or three wire nails.

STEP 4 Turn the insect hotel over and fill it with natural materials, packing it tightly with a combination of large and small pieces. Fill any gaps with moss or straw. Cover the front of the insect house with the second panel of hardware cloth; trim and staple it into place. To hide the rough edges of the hardware cloth (as on the back), cut and nail the screen molding along the edges of the frame (C).

STEP 5 Mount your insect house on a sturdy post. A natural post made from a small tree looks best, even if it is a little crooked. Screw the last piece of wood, a 13-inch (33-cm) board, onto the top of the post, using two or three screws. On a flat surface, place this board against the bottom of the bug house and secure it with four screws. The house is now solidly attached to the post. Sink the post about 18 inches (46 cm) in the ground, taking care to keep the bottom of the bug house level.

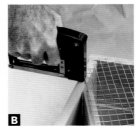

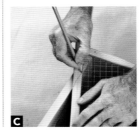

116 plant a diverse landscape

Planting a range of trees, shrubs, vines, groundcovers, and flowers is the key to attracting birds and other wildlife to your yard. Plants contribute the essentials of life: food, water, and shelter.

117 play host with an organ pipe feeder

Host a bevy of backyard birds with a feeder made from an old organ pipe.

MATERIALS

Handsaw

Vintage organ pipe or other hollow cylinder

Sandpaper

½-inch (1.25-cm) metal rod

Hacksaw

Super Glue

Epoxy adhesive

Galvanized storm collar cap and storm collar

Drill

Hammer

6-inch (15-cm) nail

Small hook-and-eye kit

1½-inch (4-cm) galvanized sheet metal

Vintage hinge pin and two small eye hooks

Rope and vintage spring

STEP 1 Using a handsaw, remove the rodlike portion of the organ pipe. Sand the cut end. Cut an 8-inch (20-cm) length of the ½-inch (1.25-cm) metal rod with a hacksaw.

STEP 2 Apply Super Glue inside the organ pipe base hole; insert the metal rod. Glue and insert the opposite end of the metal rod into the organ pipe rod so about 3 inches (8 cm) remains exposed. Spread epoxy on the storm collar cap bottom, then attach the storm collar to create a feeding dish.

STEP 3 Drill a hole through the center of feeding dish. Apply Super Glue inside the organ pipe rod or cylinder. Run the 6-inch (15-cm) nail through the dish and into the rod to attach.

STEP 4 Use a hammer to pound the metal on the top of the organ pipe flat against the pipe to form the lid. Add a hook-and-eye closure. Attach a small piece of galvanized sheet metal to the opening near the bottom of the organ pipe using Super Glue to fashion the small feeding dish.

STEP 5 Drill a hole below the small feeding dish. Apply Super Glue to the hinge pin; insert the hinge pin into the hole to create a perch. Attach an eye hook to one side of the organ pipe, centering it about 1 inch (2.5 cm) from the top. Repeat on the opposite side.

STEP 6 Thread an appropriate length of rope through the eye hooks and tie a knot about 8 inches (20 cm) above the feeder. Slip the vintage spring onto the rope. Hang your bird feeder.

118 feed a hummingbird by hand

Attract winged wonders even to the smallest spaces. Hand-feeding hummingbirds is possible—with patience.

The first step in attracting hummingbirds to your yard is by placing several sugar-water feeders around it.

As the hummingbird traffic in your yard increases, start quietly mingling among them so the hummingbirds get used to your presence. Even if they are scared off at first, stick with it. They'll be back—the sweet stuff is just too good to give up forever.

Once they get used to you, hold the sugar-water feeder in your hand. If you are very quiet and still, they should eventually begin to feed from the one you're holding.

When you have a good hummer turnout one day, remove all of the other feeders in your yard. Place a small feeder filled with sugar water in the palm of your hand.

Now simply go outside and wait. If you happen to have picked a day with a fair number of tiny diners visiting—and you remove the other food sources—you'll have a better chance of feeling the flutter of a hummingbird in your hand.

119 attract hummingbirds with sage

The brilliant blooms of sage (Salvia spp.) are among the favorite flowers of these tiny birds.

FORSYTHIA SAGE (A) Spikes of brilliant yellow flowers attract migrating hummingbirds and butterflies when it blooms in mid-fall.

MEXICAN SAGE (B) The silvery foliage of this warm-weather plant is as pretty as its fuzzy blooms—but it's the flowers that draw hummingbirds.

HAIRY ROSELEAF SAGE (C) Also known as Hidalgo Roseleaf Sage, this salvia with deep pink flowers can grow up to 6 feet (1.8 m) tall and 4 feet (1.2 m) wide.

HYBRID ROSELEAF SAGE (D) Both the leaves and the fuzzy, tubular, deep-rose-pink flowers of this sage are fragrant hummingbird magnets.

COSTA RICAN BLUE SAGE (E) Large violet-blue flowers and oversize tropical-type leaves make this sage a standout in the garden.

PINEAPPLE SAGE (F) The bright-red blooms on this pineapple-scented plant draws hummingbirds like bees to honey.

VAN HOUTTE SAGE (G) This Brazilian native needs protection at temperatures below 30°F (-1°C), but it will reward you with a prolific bloom of showy deep-red flowers.

TEXAS SAGE (H) Often called the Barometer Plant in its native state, this easy-care plant bursts into bloom when the humidity rises after very dry weather.

AUTUMN SAGE (I) This petite plant—just 2 to 3 feet (60–90 cm) tall at maturity—has mint-scented leaves and blooms that can be red, pink, or orange.

BLUE BUSH SAGE (J) Excellent in containers, this long-blooming plant produces deep-blue violet flowers.

120 stir up nectar

To make nectar for hummingbird feeders, mix 4 parts water with 1 part sugar. Bring the mixture to a boil, then let it cool. Do not add red food coloring. Store extra nectar in the refrigerator up to three days. Clean and refill feeders every day to prevent mold and bacteria growth. Scrub feeders with a brush and hot water.

121 plant color in clumps

Signal that nectar is near by planting a big, bold patch of vibrant red, purple, or yellow flowers to act as a butterfly beacon. Here, *Monarda*, commonly known as bee balm (A), and *Lyrthum salicaria*, aka purple loosestrife (B), do the trick.

122 avoid using chemicals

There is no place for pesticides and herbicides in a butterfly garden. Butterflies are insects and susceptible to toxic effects of chemicals. Loosen your view on tidiness and weeds. What many gardeners consider weeds are actually host plants to caterpillars.

four ways to attract butterflies

Bright color blooms bring beauty to your garden in more than one way. The colors and shapes add visual interest, while attracting nectar-seeking butterflies. Try these varieties.

123 plant purple coneflower

The plant tolerates heat, wind, humidity, and drought. This perennial attracts butterflies, birds, and bees, but not deer.

SIZE 2 to 4 feet (60–120 cm) tall; 1½ to 2 feet (46–60 cm) wide.

REQUIREMENTS Full sun to partial shade; well-draining soil amended with compost; regular moisture for best performance; deadheading prompts reflowering.

124 sow cosmos

Grows easily from seed and develops delicate flowers in colors ranging from pink to white, purple, orange, yellow, and bicolors with wispy foliage. The flowers attract both hummingbirds and bees.

SIZE 2 to 4 feet (60–120 cm) tall; 1 to 2 feet (30–60 cm) wide.

REQUIREMENTS Full sun; tolerates most soils; needs even moisture.

125 glow with garden phlox

Light pink and white varieties that light up the evening garden prove irresistible to all varieties of butterflies.

SIZE 3 feet (1 m) tall; 2 feet (60 cm) wide.

REQUIREMENTS Partial shade to full sun; plants tolerate most soils and wind but not drought with extreme heat and high humidity.

126 grow *verbena bonariensis*

This fast grower is an outstanding plant in the summer and fall garden. Butterflies have no trouble finding the nectar-laden flower clusters.

SIZE 2 to 3 feet (60–90 cm) tall; 2 feet (60 cm) wide.

REQUIREMENTS Full sun; well-draining soil; tolerates drought and heat.

127 plant in layers

To attract birds to your garden year-round, include a mix of plantings from the ground level to the tree canopy. Various-size trees and shrubs combine to form the essential backbone of any wildlife garden. They also offer nesting sites and shelter from weather and predators. Here, arborvitae create a dark green wall of protection. Ornamental grasses such as those of giant feather grass (*Stipa gigantea*) provide seeds during winter—the toughest time of the year—and nesting materials as well as places to hide, sleep, and stay warm. The waving flowers create a sense of motion in the garden help catch the eyes of feathered friends.

mini gardens & terrariums

128 create a mossy lotus bowl

Fill a large round planter bowl with potting soil. Cut the stems of dried lotus pods (painted or natural) to 2 inches (5 cm), and insert them in the soil to create a pod pathway. Surround the pathway with assorted dried or live mosses and natural dried floral materials, such as tall okra pods, dried mushrooms, and a bell cup or two. Nestle three small preserved moss spheres in a cluster. Create a tiny arbor by bending several lengths of grapevine into an arch, wiring the vines together at the ends. Push the ends into the soil, burying them 2 to 4 inches (5–10 cm) deep. Plant with pink polka-dot plant (*Hypoestes spp.*), purple waffle plant (*Hemigraphis spp.*), and trailing variegated vinca. Tuck a friendly frog figurine in the bell cup, and set the planter in a shady spot. Mist live mosses frequently and don't let planter dry out completely.

129 grow a fern forest

A shallow wooden pedestal bowl and a large round wire tray are the foundation pieces for this charming tableau that features a variety of leafy ferns.

Large round basket tray

Dried or live mosses

Potting soil

Wood slice for crafting

Pedestal bowl

Miniature house

3 to 5 small ferns (we used, clockwise from top: *Pteris quadriaurata* 'Tricolor,' *Asplenium* 'Crispy Wave,' *P. ensiformis* 'Evergemiensis,' and *P. cretica* var. *albolineata*)

Small pebbles, such as aquarium rock

Bamboo skewers

Super Glue

Bits of bark and twigs

Decorative elements, such as toadstools, tiny furniture, and animals

STEP 1 Begin by lining the basket edges with dried or live mosses, then fill it to just below the rim with potting soil. Pat the soil gently in place and level it, then lay a wood slice on the soil to create a sturdy base for the pedestal bowl.

STEP 2 Top the bowl with dried mosses and a miniature house. Plant three to five small ferns, such as the ones shown here, clockwise from top right: *Pteris quadriaurata* 'Tricolor,' *Asplenium* 'Crispy Wave,' *P. ensiformis* 'Evergemiensis,' and *P. cretica* var. *albolineata.*

STEP 3 Arrange moss over the soil, leaving a space for the path to the house, then fill the path with small pebbles (aquarium rock is perfect for this).

STEP 4 Make a ladder by gluing pieces of bamboo skewers together, then prop it in place.

STEP 5 Finally, tuck in the details: small bits of bark and twigs, decorative toadstools, tiny rustic furniture, and animals. Place in dappled light or shade and do not allow the plants to dry out.

130 dive into a pretty little pond

A square wooden planter box provides the basis for this diminutive water garden.

MATERIALS

12- to 16-inch- (30–40-cm) square, 4-inch- (10-cm-) deep wood planter box with broad, flat edges

Drill (optional)

Potting soil

Creeping thyme (*Thymus* 'Elfin')

Wood skewers, chopsticks, or long craft sticks

U-shape floral pins

Small ivy (*Hedera helix* 'Spetchley,' or another small variety)

Miniature pond

Preserved moss

Small flat river stones

Miniature arbor

Small pebbles, such as aquarium rock

Miniature Adirondack chairs

Tiny potted plants

STEP 1 If the box does not have drainage holes, drill two or three before beginning the project. Fill the box with potting soil up to 1 inch (2.5 cm) from the rim, pressing gently to level.

STEP 2 Plant a creeping thyme (*Thymus* 'Elfin' or other low creeping variety) in each corner. Cut wood skewers, chopsticks, or long craft sticks to size to create edging for the pebbles and pond, and pin them in place with U-shape floral pins.

STEP 3 Plant a small ivy (*Hedera helix* 'Spetchley' or another small variety) in one corner of the center section, trimming it to one or two long stems. Settle a miniature pond in the center, tucking preserved moss around it.

STEP 4 Arrange small flat river stones on the moss around the pond. Press a miniature arbor in place over the pond, then twine the ivy through one side of the arbor.

STEP 5 After all is placed to your liking, carefully arrange the pebbles, filling the area at least ¼ inch (6 mm) deep. A pair of small Adirondack chairs and tiny potted plants make it homey and inviting. Keep your little pond in a bright light, while protecting it from hot afternoon sun. Be sure to water the plants regularly.

131 turn a printer's tray into a planter

Vintage printer's trays are perfect for displaying tiny plants and nature's curiosities. Sun and water will degrade the wood over time, so choose your tray accordingly. Collect various dried mosses and lichen, a small bottle or vase, pretty pebbles, shells, and other natural materials. Fill some, but not all, the sections with your precious finds, making a pleasing arrangement across the tray. Plant small succulents, such as low sedum varieties and hens and chicks (*Sempervivum spp.*), in a few of the sections, and rest air plants (*Tillandsia spp.*) in others. Mist air plants and water succulents sparingly once a week.

132
revamp
a relic

Transform a cracked pitcher or tall vase into a succulent-laden "antiquity." If you need to create a suitable pot, draw a line where you want the break, then use a masonry bit to drill small holes every ¼ inch (6 mm) along the line. Use a hammer to gently remove pieces. If you accidentally take too much, you can glue some sections back in place. If your pot doesn't have a drainage hole, drill a ½-inch (1.25-cm) hole in the base. Fill the pot with soil formulated for cacti and succulents, and, starting at the bottom, tuck in trailing sedum, green and purple *Sempervivum*, and other succulents. Insert large pottery shards to hold plants in place, creating layers of soil and plants from bottom to top.

133 picnic in the pines

Transport yourself to a cabin in the forest with a picnic basket outfitted for planting.

MATERIALS

Picnic basket

Plastic sheet or bag

Screwdriver (optional)

Potting soil

Two small rounded dwarf conifers (We used *Chamaecyparis pisifera* 'Fairy Puff.')

One taller, narrow conifer (such as *C. pisifera* 'Blue Moon')

Dried or live mosses

Miniature house

Small twigs, approximately 5 inches (13 cm) long

Flat river stones

Toothpick

Green reindeer moss

Miniature woodland creature

STEP 1 Line the basket with the plastic sheet or bag. If you plan to display the basket outdoors where rain will fall, poke a few drainage holes in the bottom of the plastic with a screwdriver.

STEP 2 Fill the plastic-lined basket with potting soil. Trim the plastic just above the soil line. Plant your three conifers, pressing the soil firmly around their roots.

STEP 3 Cover the soil with mosses. Place miniature house in the center. Push the twigs into the soil all around the edge of the basket to create a fence, leaving a gap for the path to the house.

STEP 4 Add river stones to form a path. Use the toothpick to tuck small clumps of reindeer moss firmly around the stones and wherever you want to cover edges and corners with greenery.

STEP 5 Complete your mini cabin scene with a woodland creature.

134 compose a tabletop woodland garden

This low-growing garden brings the intrigue of a forest floor to a table—indoors or out—where details can be viewed from all sides.

MATERIALS

Tray

Preserved moss

Hot-glue gun and glue sticks or floral adhesive

Driftwood

Moss ribbon

Dried lichen

Tree fern pot

Plants: air plant, fern, violet, begonia, *Peperomia*, *Pilea*, Chinese primrose

Floral wire

Spanish moss

Miniature accessories, such as dried seedpods, pinecones, and tiny figurines

Floral clay

STEP 1 Make a watertight base for your tabletop garden by covering a metal or plastic tray with a sheet of preserved moss. Conceal the edges of the tray with bits of moss, holding the moss in place with dabs of hot glue or floral adhesive (A).

STEP 2 Enhance the earthiness of the driftwood by attaching lengths of moss or moss ribbon and dried lichen here and there with hot glue (B). Place the driftwood on the tray.

STEP 3 Before adding a plant to your tabletop garden, transplant a small specimen into a tree fern pot (C). The fibrous container will provide a well-draining home for a plant with a small root ball. Alternatively, wrap the plant's nursery pot with moss, using floral wire to secure it. Cover any bare soil with Spanish moss.

STEP 4 Add miniature accessories in scale with the plants to complete the illusion of a woodland garden (D). Use a pinch of floral clay to attach a cone, seedpod, and tiny frog or other figurine to the driftwood.

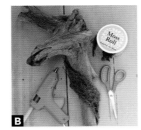

135 forage for materials

This woodland scene will last for months when placed in bright indirect light and watered regularly. Find materials for your woodland tabletop garden in crafts stores, on the internet, or in a garden center. Forage for twigs, live moss, and other treasures from nature in your yard. Little potted ferns, begonias, and other low-light houseplants work well for a tabletop garden, as will most air plants (*Tillandsia*). Young perennials, such as violets and primroses, destined for a woodland or shade garden outside, can spend a few weeks indoors as long as they receive adequate sunlight. Although plants grow slowly with their roots confined, they will eventually need to be repotted and moved to permanent quarters indoors or in the garden.

136 pack a trunk with plants

Sun-loving dwarf conifers make the scene in this large-scale planting.

MATERIALS

Log planter

Flagstone pieces

Sphagnum moss

Potting mix for conifers

Dwarf conifers, such as creeping juniper, dwarf Alberta spruce, and Hinoki cypress

Drought-tolerant groundcovers, such as cinquefoil, and assorted thyme varieties

Diascia 'Sun Chimes Coral'

English lavender (*Lavandula angustifolia*)

Fine bark mulch

STEP 1 Fill the openings at the ends of the planter with small stacked flagstones (A). Form planting tiers by adding a stone retaining wall inside the planter, if you wish.

STEP 2 Line the bottom of the log with sphagnum moss. Fill the planter with well-draining potting mix for conifers (B).

STEP 3 Position and plant all plants (C), such as cinquefoil, thyme, *Diascia* 'Sun Chimes Coral,' and English lavender. Enhance the planter with decorative rocks, especially if it is necessary to help it balance securely.

STEP 4 Cover exposed potting mix with a thin layer of fine bark mulch. Between waterings, allow the soil to dry. In cold climates, insulate the planter with leaves and cover with burlap in winter. Fertilize the plants annually.

137 plant a miniature conifer garden

Pot single specimens or combine them for a tiny landscape.

MATERIALS

Liquid fertilizer

Bowl of water

Miniature conifers in varying forms: *Picea glauca* 'Jean's Dilly,' and *Chamaecyparis pisifera* 'Tsukumo'

Shallow container with drainage holes

Fine screen

Bonsai soil (good drainage mix)

Small perennial (we used a chartreuse *Heuchera*)

Chopstick

A decorative rock

Gravel

Sheet moss

STEP 1 Add a few drops of liquid fertilizer to the bowl of water, and soak the conifer roots for five minutes.

STEP 2 Cover the holes of the container with a fine screen to retain the soil and prevent clogging (A).

STEP 3 Fill the bottom of the container with a layer of the bonsai soil mix (B).

STEP 4 Spread the roots of the conifer and place the plant on the soil (C). Gently press soil over the roots.

STEP 5 Add any other plants (such as a chartreuse *Heuchera*), covering the roots with additional soil. Use a chopstick to tap around plant roots to fill pockets with soil (D).

STEP 6 Add a decorative rock (E). Cover the soil with gravel and sheet moss to prevent evaporation (F).

138 make a mini succulent garden

Plant a charming little desert landscape full of miniature delights.

MATERIALS

1-foot (30-cm) terra-cotta pot saucer, with or without drainage holes

Cactus mix potting soil

Miniature garden furnishings, such as a wheelbarrow, arbor, chair, urn, and/or cat

Finely crushed rock or tiny pebbles

Succulents with small leaves: watch-chain crassula, delicate sedums, small stacked crassulas, *Sedum rubrotinctum*, and *Crassula tetragona* (to suggest trees)

STEP 1 Fill the terra-cotta pot saucer with potting mix to ½ inch (1.25 cm) below the rim. Secure the miniature arbor about 1 inch (2.5 cm) inside the rim of the saucer.

STEP 2 Create a pathway of finely crushed rock or pebbles that curves from the lower right of the saucer through the miniature arbor (A).

STEP 3 Pinch the top ½ inch (1.25 cm) of the sedums so you can insert their rosettes or tips into the soil, between the pathway and rim, to create a lush and verdant garden of your liking (B).

STEP 4 Add accents. Here, we filled a mini wheelbarrow with soil and planted it with cuttings. We used the top 3 to 4 inches (8–10 cm) of *Crassula tetragona* for a little tree (C), and we positioned a chair beneath the arbor and topped it with a tiny sleeping cat.

A

B

C

139 hang a cactus garden

Bring color and texture to a dark corner with this miniaturized desert globe.

MATERIALS

8-inch (20-cm) open-front glass globe terrarium

Jar ring (to hold it during assembly)

Sand

Potting soil

Tiny shovel

Plants (clockwise from top left): rainbow hedgehog cactus, Echeveria 'Lola,' Tanzanian zipper plant, *Graptosedum* 'Alpenglow,' *Graptoveria* 'Moonglow,' and *Opuntia fragilis*

Long tweezers

Syringe

Funnel

Spoon

White pebbles

Soft paintbrush

STEP 1 Set the glass globe on the jar ring, then fill it one-fourth with sand and make a well in it; add potting soil to the center (A).

STEP 2 Add rooted succulents or cuttings as though planting a garden bed. Use long tweezers to position items where fingers can't reach (B).

STEP 3 Settle the roots and soil with a syringe or two full of water (about 1 ounce [30 mL]) (C).

STEP 4 Use a funnel or spoon to distribute sand around the base of your plants, concealing the soil (D). A different-color sand, when viewed through the glass, will create intriguing striation.

STEP 5 Strew pebbles to visually connect the plants with the sand (E). Use a soft paintbrush to clean the plants.

A

B

C

D

E

140 begin with bonsai

Learn the art of bonsai in just three easy steps.

MATERIALS

Small conifer (we used *Juniperus squamata* 'Blue Star')

Small pruners

Water in a spray bottle

Shallow pot

Bonsai soil

Gravel or moss

Copper wire

Wire cutters

STEP 1 Remove the plant from its nursery container, and cut off the bottom two-thirds of the root ball. Rake through the soil on the surface to expose the roots. Moisten the roots using the spray bottle (A).

STEP 2 Remove any branches that are dead or distract from the vision you have for your tree (B). Cut away any dead roots and large roots that will interfere with potting. Position the plant in your shallow pot, and work the soil in well around the roots. Top the soil with gravel or moss. Water well.

STEP 3 Decide which branches would benefit from shaping. Wrap wire around branches snugly but not so tightly that it inhibits growth. Trim off excess wire with wire cutters. Gently bend branches into desired shape. In about three months, when the branch has grown accustomed to its new shape, remove the wire from the tree.

A

B

141 care for dwarf conifers

Add interest to your yard with a collection of tiny trees in pots. Here's how to keep them healthy.

POT THEM RIGHT Plant conifers in containers with drainage holes and be sure to use a high-quality, well-draining soil.

CHOOSE HEARTY PLANTS Select container plants that can withstand cold greater than what you experience in your area.

GIVE IT BRIGHT LIGHT During the growing season, place conifer containers in the type of sunlight indicated on each plant's information tag. For most conifers, that means full sun.

WATER FOR THE WEATHER In the heat of the summer or in drying winds, water the containers daily. In cool months, water the conifers regularly but less frequently (every 1 to 2 weeks). It's important that conifers are fully hydrated—but not soggy—when freezing weather arrives. Water plants as needed during winter warm spells.

FERTILIZE Use a liquid fertilizer regularly when watering throughout the growing season, starting in late winter and ending in mid- to late summer.

SHAPE IT Trim the plants to achieve the desired form. You can learn bonsai techniques at a local botanical garden or conservatory.

CARE IN WINTER Overwinter the containers along a protected northern side of the house, out of direct sunlight and winds. If temperatures drop below 0°F (–18°C), temporarily store containers in an unheated garage. Do not overwinter conifers indoors where it is heated.

142 create a fairy forest

Use salvaged and natural materials to dream up a miniature woodland wonderland.

LANDSCAPE (A) Set the stage for enchanting details by arranging miniature cottages in a wooded nook of your garden. Create paths between vignettes with moss and pebbles

MADE FOR SHADE (B) Gather an assortment of things, trying not to be too literal about shapes and composition. Anything can become ingredients for fairy people, furniture, or features. Here, a tiny umbrella table and chairs come to life using a cast-off gear as the base and a small metal baking mold as the umbrella. Wine corks provide comfy seating.

WATER FEATURE (C) Glass ramekins become little ponds in the garden.

SAND BOX (D) A tire from an old toy truck makes a perfect sand box for this playful fairy.

FAIRY WINGS (E) Skeleton leaves become gossamer-light wings for fairies but could also become curtains, blankets, capes, and more.

GREEN PILLOWS (F) A cushion of moss makes fairy furniture more comfortable.

GARDEN'S EDGE (G) Walls of outdoor rooms needn't reach to the sky—they can be outlined with anything, such as wine corks.

143 bottle up a nature scene

The elements in this terrarium are highly adaptable so you can create the scene of your dreams.

MATERIALS

Clear glass container with an opening large enough to insert plants

Gloves

Clean ½- to ¾-inch (1.25–2-cm) pebbles

Dried sphagnum moss

Bowl

A dowel for tamping

Wooden spoon

Moistened potting soil

Terrarium plants: ferns, palm seedlings, and mini-philodendrons

Oversize tweezers

Lichen, stones, driftwood, shells, or other bits of nature

Figurines of your choosing

Turkey baster or small measuring cup with a spout

STEP 1 Make a 1- to 2-inch (2.5–5-cm) layer (depending on the size of your glassware) of pebbles in the base of the container (A).

STEP 2 Fully moisten the sphagnum moss in a bowl, and wring out excess water (B).

STEP 3 Insert a thin layer of sphagnum moss into the container and tamp it down with a dowel.

STEP 4 Spoon 1 inch (2.5 cm) of moistened soil into the container, tamping it down (C).

STEP 5 Unpot one mini plant and massage the roots to loosen them before inserting the plant into the container with a pair of tweezers (D). Carefully place it firmly into the soil. Repeat with additional plants, leaving growing room between them.

STEP 6 Add soil to fill in gaps, and tamp it to fully firm the plants in place.

STEP 7 With tweezers, insert lichen, stones, twigs, and natural objects (E). Add your figurines to the scene.

STEP 8 Add 1 to 2 tablespoons water with the turkey baster or cup. Seal the container with the stopper (F). Closed terrariums require little to no continued watering. Water only when the plants begin to look dry.

A

B

C

D

E

F

144 keep a memory alive

As a variation on #143, instead of a photo album, keep vacation memories alive by staging them in an apothecary jar. Remember bicycling in the wilderness, backpacking in the mountains, or lounging by the lake.

145 garden under glass

Miniature conservatories, sometimes called Wardian cases, have been favorites of gardeners since Victorian times. The glass enclosures are downsized versions of the elegant greenhouses in English gardens.

MATERIALS

Miniature glass conservatory with at least a 3-inch- (8-cm-) deep base

Pea gravel

Horticultural charcoal chips

Cheesecloth

Potting mix

Miniature plants

STEP 1 Cover the bottom of the conservatory's base with a 1-inch (2.5-cm) layer of pea gravel; sprinkle horticultural charcoal chips over the gravel. Cut cheesecloth to the size of the base, then place the cheesecloth on the charcoal and gravel. Cover the cheesecloth with a 1-inch (2.5-cm) layer of potting mix. Set the plant root balls on the potting mix. Fill in between the root balls with additional potting mix. Gently water plants. NOTE: If your conservatory doesn't have a built-in base, find a tray in an appropriate size to set it on. Cover the bottom of the tray with a layer of pea gravel. If it is at least 3 inches (8 cm) deep, fill it with potting mix for direct planting.

STEP 2 Set your conservatory in bright or diffused light, depending on the plant needs; avoid placing it in direct light to prevent overheating and scorching plants.

STEP 3 Check on the plants periodically and water them as needed. Remove the container's top to ventilate the plants every few days and to prevent fungal or mold problems in the humid conditions.

146 convert a cake stand into a terrarium

A cake stand with a domed glass cover becomes a tiny woodsy landscape fit for a centerpiece.

MATERIALS

Glass cake stand with lid

Moss

Stones, twigs, pinecones, and other natural objects of choice

Mister

STEP 1 Cover the platform of the cake stand with a layer of moss (A). Mound it in the center of the display for a natural appearance.

STEP 2 Add stones, twigs, pinecones, and other appealing items, arranging them as desired (B).

STEP 3 Lightly mist the arrangement, then place the glass dome over it. Mist the moss weekly or whenever it starts to feel dry (C).

project tip

147 gather moss

Use pieces of live moss gathered from your yard—not from the wild. For a more permanent display, purchase preserved sheet moss. To collect moss from the yard, carefully lift it with a small amount of soil attached. Display the moss garden away from direct sunlight.

148 create a garden globe

Combine the best of two delightful worlds—terrariums and miniature gardens—for a charming little scene that is a cinch to assemble and maintain.

MATERIALS

Small pebbles

Horticultural charcoal

8-inch (20-cm) open-front glass globe terrarium

Teaspoon

Potting soil

Two small plants: maidenhair fern, nerve plant, or succulents

Preserved moss

Small paintbrush

Colorful glass pebbles or aquarium gravel

Miniature accessories

STEP 1 Mix the small pebbles with the horticultural charcoal and pour the mixture into the bottom of the terrarium (A). Use the teaspoon to place potting soil on the pebble mixture, loading it higher at the back of the globe than at the front. Smooth and gently tamp down the soil with the spoon to make a sloped planting area that ends about 1 inch (2.5 cm) from the terrarium's opening.

STEP 2 Using the spoon as a shovel, add the two small plants to your terrarium, nestling them into the soil near the back of the globe (B). Press the soil in snugly around plant roots.

STEP 3 Moisten the preserved moss with water, and tear it into two or three pieces that will cover the bare soil (C). Press it gently into place. Use the paintbrush to clean soil particles from the inside of the globe.

STEP 4 Use the spoon to carefully arrange the colorful glass pebbles inside the globe. Place small accessories to finish the scene.

STEP 5 To water the little garden, pour a gentle stream of water directly over the crowns of the plants—not over the moss—using only 2 to 3 tablespoons water each time (D). Place your terrarium in bright, indirect sunlight. Avoid overwatering.

149 design a desert dwelling

A drywaller's pan provides a sleek cachepot for small individually potted plants, such as this collection of succulents and cacti in a south-facing window. Gravel conceals the pot rims.

150 turn a fish tank into a terrarium

A vintage fish tank picked up at a thrift shop houses this simple terrarium. The tank frames a miniature piece of forest, scaled down for ease of contemplation.

MATERIALS

Pea gravel

15×8×10-inch (38×20×25-cm) aquarium

Horticultural or activated charcoal

Vinyl window screening

Peat moss or potting soil

Norfolk island pine

Sheet moss (green-preserved moss mat)

Scissors

Sharp knife

One or two small terrarium plants

Decorative rock

STEP 1 Pour a 2-inch (5-cm) layer of pea gravel evenly across the floor of the terrarium. Distribute a ½-inch (1.25-cm) layer of horticultural charcoal over the gravel (A).

STEP 2 Cut a piece of vinyl window screen to 15×8 inches (38×20 cm), or the size of the base of your aquarium. The screen should cover the charcoal and gravel layers and prevent them from mixing with top layers; trim the screen so the edges are covered when the peat moss is added. Place the screen on the charcoal (B).

STEP 3 Add a 1-inch (2.5-cm) layer of peat moss or potting soil over the screen. Place the pine where you'd like it; off-center is a more visually appealing composition (C). Surround the pine with more peat moss or potting soil.

STEP 4 Cut the green mat of preserved moss to fit the terrarium. Into one side of the mat, cut a slit to fit around the miniature tree (D).

STEP 5 Place the moss mat inside the tank to form the top layer, opening the slit to wrap the moss around the pine (E).

STEP 6 Use a knife or box cutter to cut small slits in the sheet moss and tuck in smaller plants. Add a rock, small statue, or woodland figure (F).

quick garden tip

151 remember the charcoal

Horticultural charcoal not only preserves drainage and aeration but also helps absorb impurities in soil—a particularly important quality when planting terrariums, which are often closed systems and can be prone to disease.

plants &
planters

152 put pips in a pocket

Get a jump on spring and the thrill of planting with early show-stopping lily-of-the-valley.

MATERIALS

Prechilled lily-of-the-valley pips

Bucket for soaking pips

Warm water

Scissors

Pocket pot (at least 8 inches [20 cm] deep)

Sand

Potting mix

Soil scoop

Sphagnum moss

Plastic planter drainage material

STEP 1 Soak the pips in a bucket of warm water for an hour (A). Trim the roots, keeping them at least 4 inches (10 cm) long. Cover the bottom of the pocket pot with a 1- to 2-inch (2.5–5-cm) layer of sand. Moisten the potting mix. Scoop potting mix to just below the lowest pockets.

STEP 2 Plant several pips in each pocket, spreading the roots on the potting mix (B). Cover the roots with potting mix. Press a small handful of dampened sphagnum moss between the pips and the top of each pocket to hold the potting mix in place.

STEP 3 Use scissors to cut a 2×8-inch (5×20-cm) chunk of plastic planter drainage material and stand it in the center of the pot to create a channel that will facilitate watering and drainage (C). (You can

also make a channel by rolling wire mesh into a 2-inch- [5-cm-] diameter tube and filling it with gravel.)

STEP 4 Finish planting any remaining openings of the pot. Cover the pips with potting mix (D). Slowly water the top plantings, allowing moisture to channel into the pockets. Plants usually begin flowering within a month.

153 plant a pussy willow pot

Break out of the winter doldrums with an enchanting little weeping pussy willow tree.

MATERIALS

Container (ours is 16×10×6 inches [40×25×15 cm])

Acrylic paint

Paintbrush

Sheet plastic or tray

Cotton batting

Soil scoop

Potting soil

Dwarf weeping pussy willow (*Salix caprea* 'Pendula')

Prechilled spring-flowering bulbs (hyacinth, grape hyacinth, and dwarf iris)

Annuals (sweet alyssum and Scotch moss)

Preserved moss

Miniature decorative fencing

STEP 1 Measure the container to make sure it's deep enough to hold the willow. Paint the container and let dry. Line the bottom with a sheet of plastic (A) or set the planter on a tray to protect the tabletop from moisture.

STEP 2 Cotton batting makes an excellent liner for a small container garden. Cut the batting to fit the container and press it into place to hold the soil (B). Using a liner means you'll water less often.

STEP 3 Cover the bottom of the lined planter with soil. Slip the dwarf weeping willow out of its nursery pot and set it in the planter (C). Gently add potting soil, surrounding the tree root ball, up to 2 inches (5 cm) below the container's rim.

STEP 4 Add other plants in a pleasing arrangement of colors and textures. Include small prechilled or forced bulbs and/or annual bedding plants. Nestle their roots into the soil (D). Fill in with bits of moss, and decorate with mini fencing.

154 pick prairie flowers

Prairie gardens are among the easiest types to maintain. These hardy plants thrive in full sun and fertile, well-drained soil.

BUTTERFLY MILKWEED (A) (*Asclepias tuberosa*) A calling card for monarchs and other butterflies, butterfly milkweed is a bold prairie plant with vibrant orange flowers that grow in June and July on 1- to 2-foot- (30–60-cm-) tall stems.

CLIMBING ROSE (B) (*Rosa setigera*) The fragrant, deep-pink summer flowers of the wild climbing rose are followed by scarlet autumn foliage and cherry-red hips. Climbing rose grows 5 to 6 feet (1.5–1.8 m) tall, and its vigorous canes can be trained up a trellis.

STARRY CAMPION (C) (*Silene stellata*) Fringed white petals on starry campion lend an airy look and soften bold stands of prairie grass from June to August. Plants grow 1 to 3 feet (30–90 cm) tall.

FALSE SUNFLOWER (D) (*Heliopsis helianthoides*) Radiant as the sun, false sunflower unfurls new blossoms for weeks beginning in July. This sturdy 3- to 5-foot- (90–150-cm-) tall plant has a strong branching habit and will form a large clump of foliage and flowers.

OHIO SPIDERWORT (E) (*Tradescantia ohiensis*) A favorite nectar source, spiderwort blooms in May and June. Its pretty three-petal flowers are accompanied by grasslike foliage. Plants grow 2 to 3 feet (60–90 cm) tall, making them ideal for the edge of a prairie garden.

RATTLESNAKE-MASTER (F) (*Eryngium yuccifolium*) Growing a rambunctious 4 feet (1.2 m) tall, rattlesnake-master has prickly, round flowers and smooth, blue-green, and swordlike foliage. Take advantage of its sculptural appearance by planting it in a prominent place.

FRINGED LOOSESTRIFE (G) (*Lysimachia ciliata*) Upright or sprawling, this perennial reaches 1 to 2 feet (30–60 cm) tall, forming masses of foliage and summer blooms. Native in wetland shores and damp thickets, it prefers wet conditions. Plant it in full sun to light shade.

GOLDEN ALEXANDER (H) (*Zizia aurea*) An important nectar source for many beneficial insects, golden Alexander blooms in May on 2½-foot- (76-cm-) tall stems. Black Swallowtail caterpillars eat both the leaves and flowers.

155 try tulips

Tulip bulbs planted shoulder to shoulder in a container during the fall bloom gloriously come spring.

MATERIALS

Plastic nursery pots (we used pots about 10 inches [25 cm] tall and 10 inches [25 cm] in diameter)

Potting soil

Tulip bulbs

Plant labels

Leaf pile

Decorative pot

STEP 1 In the fall, fill a pot about one-third full of potting soil. Place tulip bulbs close together in the pot, so they just touch each other (A). In a 10-inch- (25-cm-) diameter pot, there should be room for about 20 bulbs. You can crowd the bulbs for impact as long as you allow enough room for the roots to grow.

STEP 2 Covering the bulbs, fill the pot with potting soil up to its rim to give tulips enough soil to support the flower stems as they emerge. Insert a plant label with the name of the bulb variety (B).

STEP 3 Tuck the pot into a leaf pile. Water the pot thoroughly until water drains out the pot bottom (C). You will not need to water again until spring.

STEP 4 Pile lots of autumn leaves on top and around the pot (D). Then wait until spring.

In spring, when the bulb foliage reaches about 6 inches (15 cm) tall, move the pot to a sunny spot and water well. Plop the plastic pot into a slightly larger decorative pot. Your tulips will bloom in seven to 10 days. The flowers will last up to two weeks if the days are cool.

156 grow microgreens

Microgreens add a bright burst of fresh flavor and nutrients to pizzas, salads, and sandwiches.

MATERIALS

Shallow, well-draining plastic tray

Indoor potting mix

Spray mister

Seeds (mustard greens, arugula, radishes, cress, chard, basil, cabbage, beets, or carrots)

Dish towel or empty tray

STEP 1 Fill the tray with potting mix. Lightly dampen the soil with a spray mister.

STEP 2 Generously sprinkle seeds on the damp soil to maximize space. Do not cover with soil mix.

STEP 3 Water very lightly and place a dish towel or empty tray over the top of the seeds to keep the soil warm and block light for a few days.

STEP 4 After the seeds sprout, remove the cover and water daily (watering from the bottom works best). Sprouts need six to eight hours of light a day.

STEP 5 Harvest! Most microgreens are tastiest when they are 1 to 2 inches (2.5–5 cm) tall. Gently take a handful and cut near the base with sharp scissors.

157 start an indoor herb garden

Peppermint, spearmint, lemongrass, parsley, oregano, thyme, and rosemary are among the easiest herbs to grow indoors.

MATERIALS

Small pots or other containers with drainage

Potting soil

Herbs seeds or small herb plants

Tray

Bag of small pebbles

Mister (optional)

Liquid fertilizer

STEP 1 Start with a small pot or other container with drainage.

STEP 2 Fill with potting soil and add water so the soil is slightly damp. Sow seeds or transplant existing herbs (either purchased or propagated) into the container.

STEP 3 Set in a location with six to eight hours of light a day and good air flow.

STEP 4 Create humidity by setting your herb containers in a tray of small pebbles and filling the tray with water. Place the pots on top of the pebbles, making sure the container bottoms don't directly touch the water. The evaporation will humidify your plants. You also can mist the plants every few days.

STEP 5 Fertilize every 10 days or so with diluted liquid fertilizer, such as a fish emulsion.

158 roll seed bombs

These are as fun to make as mud pies—and they grow beautiful clusters of flowers!

MATERIALS

Fresh clay soil or dried clay

Compost

Water

Annual or wildflower
 seeds

Drying rack

Plant labels (optional)

STEP 1 If you don't have clay soil in your area, purchase dried clay from a local ceramics supplier or online source. Mix 2 parts dried clay with 1 part compost. Add enough water to make a soft and malleable consistency (A).

STEP 2 Mix the clay with your hands or stir it until it is the proper consistency for rolling (B). If clay is too runny, add dried clay; if it is too stiff, add water.

STEP 3 Roll the soft clay between your palms to form walnut-size balls (about 1 inch [2.5 cm] in diameter) (C).

STEP 4 Press 20 to 30 seeds into each clay ball. Reshape the ball, working the seeds into the clay. Set the balls on a rack to dry for several days in a warm airy place (D). Store away from heat and moisture. Label seed balls, if desired.

STEP 5 Simply toss in a sunny spot or plant in the ground. Or, use one seed ball per small container. To gift, wrap in fabric or tissue paper and tie with a bow. Attach a label with planting instructions.

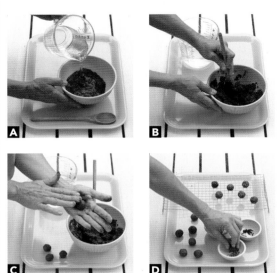

four ways to captivate your senses

The sensory pleasures of the garden are numerous. The combination of plants in each of these planters is a concentrated appeal to your sense of sight, smell, touch, and taste.

159 taste

Savor the flavors of edible flowers and herbs.

CONTAINER 16-inch- (40-cm-) square wooden box

FLOWERS Miniature rose (*Rosa*), Dill (*Anethum graveolens*), Grape tomato, Mint (*Mentha spp.*), Zinnia, Parsley (*Petroselinum crispum*), Dianthus, Nasturtium (*Tropaeolum*), Sweet potato vine (*Ipomoea batatas*), Sage (*Salvia* 'Tricolor'), Viola

160 smell

Take a deep breath to brighten your day.

CONTAINER 15-inch- (38-cm-) diameter terra-cotta pot and 18-inch- (46-cm-) wide market basket

FLOWERS Eucalyptus, Heliotrope (*Heliotropium spp.*), Scented geranium 'Attar of Roses' (*Pelargonium*), Lavender (*Lavandula angustifolia*), Sweet alyssum (*Lobularia maritima*), *Plectranthus ciliatus* 'Vanilla Twist,' *Lobelia erinus*

161 look

Add vivid color to a dull spot or dark corner.

CONTAINER 28-inch- (70-cm-) wide vintage porcelain baby bathtub

FLOWERS *Salvia farinacea* 'Victoria Blue,' Zinnia 'Profusion Orange,' 'Profusion Pink,' *Osteospermum* 'Symphony,' Sweet alyssum (*Lobularia maritima*), *Sanvitalia, Lobelia erinus* 'Compact Blue'

162 touch

Run your fingers over fuzzy and smooth textures.

CONTAINER 15-inch- (38-cm-) diameter vintage enamel pot

FLOWERS Northern sea oats (*Chasmanthium latifolium*), Fiber optic grass (*Scirpus cernuus*), Ageratum 'Artist Blue,' Silver sage (*Salvia argentea*), Chenille plant (*Acalypha hispida*), Lavender (*Lavandula angustifolia*), *Helichrysum petiolare* 'Lemon Licorice'

163 plant an amaryllis pot

This big bulb has supersize blooms that make for a long-running show.

MATERIALS

Potting mix

Tub (to mix potting soil)

Container with drainage hole (6-inch [15-cm] for one bulb, 10- to 12-inch [25–30-cm] for groups of three bulbs)

Small piece of mesh screen

Amaryllis bulb(s)

STEP 1 Place potting mix in a tub and sprinkle with lukewarm water, stirring until moist but not soggy. Cover the container's drainage hole with a mesh screen to keep soil from escaping (A).

STEP 2 Fill the container halfway with damp potting mix (B).

STEP 3 Nestle the bulb into the center of the container (C). If you plant more than one amaryllis in the same container, place bulbs shoulder to shoulder. (The bulbs should be firm and plump with healthy roots at the bases.)

STEP 4 Fill in with more potting mix, leaving the top third of the bulb uncovered (D). Tamp firmly and gently around the bulb to settle the potting mix. Water well, being careful not to wet the exposed top of the bulb. Label to remember the variety name.

STEP 5 Place in a sunny spot and water when the potting mix begins to dry. The bulbs will flower about 5 to 6 weeks after planting.

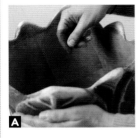
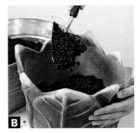

164 shake up cocktails with fresh herbs

Infuse your cocktails with the fresh flavors of garden herbs.

MATERIALS

Large container

Potting soil

Basil plant

Lavender plant

Rosemary plant

Wine corks

Tree branch labels

Permanent marker

STEP 1 Fill the bottom half of the container with potting soil; plant basil, lavender, and rosemary—or other herbs of your choice (A). Plant the herbs 1 to 2 inches (2.5–5 cm) below the lip of the container, allowing room for a dense layer of corks. Continue to fill the container with potting soil, surrounding the new plantings.

STEP 2 Cover the exposed potting soil with a thick layer of wine corks to hold in moisture (B).

STEP 3 Write the plant names on the labels using a permanent marker (C). NOTE: If you're unable to find tree branch labels, make your own from a fallen or pruned tree limb. Carefully cut a tree branch into ¼- to ½-inch- (6–12-mm) thick sections. Wearing garden gloves for protection, use a nail or ice pick to make a hole on the edge. (A drill with a small bit will also work.) Insert a bamboo skewer as the stake.

165 add a pop of color with coleus

Take an eye-catching coleus to new heights with simple trimming and staking techniques.

MATERIALS

Upright coleus with a strong central stem

Planter (we used an 8-inch [20-cm] pot)

Potting soil

Small pruning snips

2-foot (60-cm) bamboo stake

6 twist ties or short lengths of garden twine

STEP 1 Plant the coleus in the pot, no deeper than it was in its original pot, pressing the soil firmly around the roots (A).

STEP 2 Starting at the soil line, clip off all leaves on the bottom two-thirds of the stem (B).

STEP 3 Carefully insert the bamboo stake next to the plant stem, pushing it to the bottom of the pot. Starting about 2 inches (5 cm) above the soil line, wrap one twist tie around the stake then gently around the stem. The tie should make a figure eight around the stake and stem. Repeat the procedure every 2 to 3 inches (5–8 cm) up the stem (C). Reserve the remaining ties to use as the plant grows. Water your standard well, and continue to care for it as described on its tag.

STEP 4 As the plant grows, snip off any new leaves that appear on the lower stem and add more ties to the top growth to protect it from wind damage (D).

STEP 5 When the plant reaches the top of the stake (or when it reaches desired height), snip off the tip of the central stem (E) to force new growth below that cut and eventually give the plant a rounder, fuller appearance. As the plant grows, trim the tips of the side stems to shape the plant. Protect the standard from wind and heavy rain.

project tip

166 pinch off blooms

Coleus produces charming little flowers toward the end of the growing season. The plants turns leggy as it blooms, however. To keep the plant bushy and compact, pinch off the flower spikes as they appear.

167 take a trip to the tropics

Cultivate an oasis with a simple water garden of lush, low-maintenance plantings.

MATERIALS

Large nonporous container, without a drainage hole

Potting soil

Pond plants or plants that tolerate getting their "feet" wet (we used 'Mojito' elephant ear, Mexican petunia, and a trailing pond plant)

Gravel

Nontoxic mosquito control product

Plant fertilizer

STEP 1 Fill the container with enough potting soil for plants to sit about 1 to 2 inches (2.5–5 cm) below the rim. Add plants, then fill in around the root balls with more potting soil (A).

STEP 2 Top the potting soil with a thick layer of gravel to keep the plants weighted down and to prevent the soil from floating (B).

STEP 3 Add nontoxic mosquito control product to prevent mosquito larvae (C).

STEP 4 Water the newly planted container, filling to the rim if desired, and replenish as needed (D). Many tropicals are heavy feeders, so fertilize often.

168 multiply your plants

Make more of your favorite plants with cuttings and divisions. In short order, you'll have extras to share.

MATERIALS

Coleus

Scissors

Small containers

Potting soil

Butterfly bush (*Buddleja*)

Vermiculite

Small flowerpot

Plastic bag

Daylilies

Spade

STEP 1 Cut a 5- to 8-inch- (13–20-cm-) long coleus stem. Remove any leaves that will be underwater and submerge the cut end in a container filled with water (A). Place the container in a sunny window and expect roots to form in about a week. After several roots form, plant the cutting in quality potting soil.

STEP 2 Cut a 4- to 6-inch- (10–15-cm-) long young stem tip off a healthy butterfly bush (*Buddleja*). Place the cutting in moistened vermiculite in a small flowerpot and water well (B). Create a humid environment by enclosing the potted cutting in a plastic bag. Place the bagged cutting in indirect light. Roots will form in one to two weeks. Transplant rooted cuttings into the garden or quality potting soil.

STEP 3 Dig up an entire daylily clump. Using a spade, sever it into sections that have ample roots in relation to the foliage (the average mature daylily clump can be divided into four sections) (C). Replant the divisions, watering them regularly for several weeks.

A

B

C

169 plant a repeating rose

The world of garden roses has evolved to include many new varieties that are not only tough and disease-resistant, but that also bloom repeatedly throughout the growing season.

MATERIALS

Shovel or spade

Drop cloth or tarp

Potted reblooming shrub rose

Watering can or hose

Mulch

STEP 1 Choose a spot for your shrub rose that receives at least six hours of direct sunlight every day and has good drainage. The planting area should be at least 2 feet (60 cm) in diameter, with room to expand as the rose grows—up to 4 feet (1.2 m) in diameter at maturity. Cut out the bed outline with a sharp shovel or spade, digging straight down at least 6 inches (15 cm) (A). Spread out the drop cloth or tarp nearby.

STEP 2 Cut horizontally through the soil, digging out sections of turf 4 to 5 inches (10–13 cm) thick, including the roots (B).

Set turf aside on the drop cloth to minimize cleanup and make it easier to transport the turf for lawn patching or to the compost bin.

STEP 3 Use a shovel to loosen the soil in the planting area before digging a hole. As you remove soil, place it on the tarp. (You'll need reserved soil to finish the job.) Dig the hole deep enough to plant the rose at approximately the same depth as the pot. To check for proper depth, set the pot in the hole and lay your shovel handle across the hole and the pot; when the shovel's handle rests across the pot and the

edges of the bed, it's the right depth (C).

STEP 4 Hold the pot over the planting hole, grasp the rose carefully just above the soil line (watch for thorns!), and carefully slide the rose out of the pot (D). Potted roses often have fertilizer granules mixed into the soil—be sure these end up in the hole near the roots. Set the rose firmly into the hole and check to make sure it is straight and level.

STEP 5 Backfill the hole with the soil you've reserved on the tarp (E). Press soil firmly around the roots to eliminate any air pockets. Add mulch; water well.

A

B

C

D

E

project tip

170 pick the perfect rose

The rose for this project is *Rosa* 'Home Run,' which has true red petals and deep green foliage that resists black spots and powdery mildew. Here are three more disease-resistant, hardy shrub roses that rebloom throughout the summer.

'KISS ME' This sweetly fragrant variety bears large two-tone pink blooms.

'ALL THE RAGE' Their coral buds become apricot blossoms with yellow centers.

'THE MAYFLOWER' These fragrant English old-rose style blooms have luscious deep-pink petals.

171 restart your succulents

Rejuvenate so-so succulents with a simple nip and tuck.

MATERIALS

Overgrown succulent plants, including various species such as crassula, aeonium, echeveria, or sedum

Sharp garden snips

Clean pot

Potting soil formulated for cacti and succulents

Soil scoop or trowel

Pea gravel or polished pebbles

STEP 1 For plants that are lanky and trailing, such as this *Sedum adolphii* (A), use the snips to make a clean cut 2 to 4 inches (5–10 cm) from the plant's healthy growing tip. Remove all leaves from the bottom third of the stem.

STEP 2 Any plants that seem to be in a tidy clump with healthy roots, such as this *Echeveria 'Perle Von Nurnberg'* (B), can be carefully dug up and divided or repotted.

STEP 3 Remove any dried leaves, or snip the stems of the plant to create new cuttings instead.

STEP 3 Fill the new pot to within 1 inch (2.5 cm) of the rim with the succulent potting mix; moisten thoroughly. Carefully transplant any rooted clumps first, pressing the soil firmly around the roots. Insert cuttings into the soil up to the first set of leaves, taking care not to snap off the stems while planting (C). Allow at least 2 inches (5 cm) between each plant to have room to grow.

STEP 5 Top the soil with pea gravel for a finished look (D) and to keep soil from splashing onto plant leaves when

watering. Move the pot to an area with bright but indirect light for two to three weeks. Don't allow the soil to dry out completely while cuttings are forming new roots, but don't keep it soggy—just barely damp soil is fine at this stage. Also, do not allow water to accumulate in the pot saucer.

STEP 6 When the plants have formed roots—holding tight to the soil when wiggled—move the pot into direct light (morning sun is best) and cut back on watering. Let the soil become dry before watering again.

quick garden tip

172 care for succulents

A primary reason for the popularity of succulents is that they can survive gardener neglect. As long as they have good drainage and don't get overwatered, most potted succulents can sit in the sun for days without any attention. Many are native to areas that never freeze in winter, forcing many gardeners to overwinter their favorite succulents indoors. Check plant information tags to determine how much cold they can tolerate.

173 grow a bouquet

Be your own florist—plant seeds for a mixed bouquet in your garden.

MATERIALS

3 or 4 packets of annual flower seeds (we used sunflower, zinnia, and two types of cosmos)

Pruners

STEP 1 After selecting annuals that have a similar planting depth and mature within one to two weeks of each other, thoroughly mix the seeds in your hand or a small bowl (A). Then scatter them in a planting furrow.

STEP 2 When harvesting, snip away spent flowers a little bit below the flower head to encourage new blossoms to develop (B).

STEP 3 When you arrange flowers, make a fresh cut at the end of each stem before placing it in water (C) to encourage water uptake, hydrating the flower to last longer.

quick garden tip

174 prolong the beauty

Make floral preservative by combining 2 tablespoons white vinegar, 2 teaspoons sugar, and ½ teaspoon bleach in 1 quart (1 L) of water. Pour the mixture into your vase and enjoy long-lasting flowers.

175 add a twist of lemon

Plant a lemon-scented garden in a basket, then see how many ways you can use the harvests.

STEP 1 Seal a 19-inch- (48-cm-) diameter basket with exterior polyurethane. Brush on several coats of sealant, allowing it to dry between applications (A).

STEP 2 Line the basket with a large piece of burlap or landscape fabric to help it hold soil. Fill the container with compost-enriched potting mix (B).

STEP 3 Add *Pelargonium* 'Mabel Grey,' lemon basil (*Ocimum* × *citriodorum*), lemon balm (*Melissa officinalis*), lemon thyme (*Thymus* × *citriodorus*), lemon mint ('Utility Citrus Kitchen' *mentha*), *Pelargonium* 'French Lace,' lemon verbena, and (*Aloysia triphylla*). Leave room between plants for growth (C). Water the plantings thoroughly. During hot, dry weather, water every day.

176 pull up a chair

Repurpose a run-down garage-sale find into a whimsical planter.

MATERIALS

Chair
Screwdriver
Paint
Paintbrush
Polyurethane spray
Stapler
Chicken wire
Coconut-fiber liner
Trowel
Potting soil
Plants
Embellishments
 (optional)

STEP 1 Using a screwdriver, remove the seat of the chair, along with any horizontal reinforcements, so the seat is completely open (A). Paint the chair the desired color and protect it with a clear polyurethane spray.

STEP 2 Staple chicken wire to create a "basket" in the seat of the chair (B).

STEP 3 Cover the chicken wire with coconut-fiber lining, and fill with potting soil (C).

STEP 4 Firmly pack the planter with a variety of colorful blossoms (D). Water well. Personalize the chair with whimsical embellishments, and enjoy!

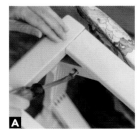

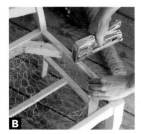

177 light things up with a lamp planter

Turn a cast-off lamp into a clever display of flowers and foliage.

MATERIALS

Hanging basket or other planting container

Lamp

Lineman's pliers or wire cutters

Steel wool

All-purpose primer

Spray paint

Copper wire and/or metal epoxy

Coconut-fiber liner

Plants

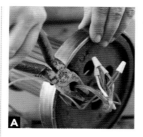

STEP 1 If you are using a hanging basket, remove the hanging hardware and chains. If using another container, drill drainage holes if it has none. Snip wiring from the lamp base. Use lineman's pliers or wire cutters to cut off the lamp cord and any other visible wiring (A). Remove the lightbulb, socket, and shade too.

STEP 2 Scuff the lamp base. Rub away loose paint or rust with steel wool to create a clean surface for primer and paint (B). Apply primer. Use a primer appropriate to your lamp base material. Let dry.

STEP 3 For easiest application, spray-paint the lamp base (C). If you would like the fixture to blend into the garden, paint it green or brown; to draw attention to your planter, use a bold color.

STEP 4 Using copper wire and pliers, attach the basket to the lamp (D). Different lamps call for different methods of attaching the planting vessels. In addition to or instead of copper wire, try metal epoxy; the gluelike substance works best on a large, uniform surface. Line the planter with coconut fiber, then plant.

178 take a new post

Turn a new wire hanging basket and a salvaged porch post into a mounted garden focal point.

MATERIALS

Saw

Salvaged porch post

Mounting kit with 9-inch- (23-cm-) diameter metal plate and open-bottom box

Drill

Wood screws

Quick-set concrete

16-inch- (40-cm-) diameter heavy-gauge wire basket with coconut-fiber liner

Plants

STEP 1 Determine the height for your planter. Cut a portion off the top of the post, if necessary (A).

STEP 2 Slide the metal box that supports the mounting plate over the top of the post (B).

STEP 3 Secure the box in place with wood screws (C). Anchor the post in a concrete base. It should be 12 to 18 inches (30–46 cm) underground to extend below the frost line.

STEP 4 Once the post is in place, center the wire basket on top of the plate. Rotate the basket until it locks into the gripping clips (D).

STEP 5 Plant with an array of leafy foliage, like you see here.

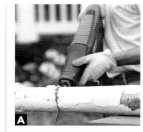

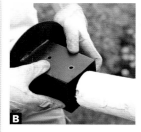

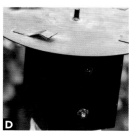

179 plant a patch that pops

Growing popcorn is as easy as popping the tasty kernels.

MATERIALS

Shovel or tiller

Fertilizer, such as aged manure

Hoe

Ruler or tape measure

Popcorn seeds

Rain gauge

STEP 1 Loosen the soil with either a shovel or tiller, working in aged manure or 12-12-12 organic fertilizer as you turn the soil (A).

STEP 2 Create a grid by carving small trenches or small holes in the soil with your hoe. Space rows 1 foot (30 cm) apart. Place one seed every 1 foot (30 cm) (B). Cover with 1 inch (2.5 cm) of soil; water with a gentle spray. If it's extremely hot, plant the kernels a little deeper—up to 2 inches (5 cm) below the surface.

STEP 3 Water plants 1 to 2 inches (2.5–5 cm) a week. You can measure water by using a rain gauge set in your garden (C). If rainfall is less than an inch, you'll need to supplement. After the popcorn sprouts, feed seedlings with an organic fertilizer.

STEP 4 At the end of the growing season, the cornstalks will turn brown, and the kernels will begin to dry and harden. When the ears of corn start to point downward, they are ready to pick. Twist each ear to separate it from the stalk (D). Make sure your popcorn kernels are completely dry by picking off a few kernels

and tossing them into hot oil in a pan. If the popcorn is ready, it will pop. If it doesn't pop, lay the remaining corn in a single layer in a dry, protected space (such as a basement or garage) until hardened.

180 pot your crops

Garden-fresh greens look beautiful planted in a pot and produce a harvest you can count on for months of salads and stir-fries.

MATERIALS

18-inch (46-cm) pot

Potting soil

Fertilizer

Six to eight 4-inch (10-cm) potted plants

Flowers (optional)

STEP 1 Fill the pot so it is almost full with potting soil, then sprinkle with fertilizer. Organic fertilizer pellets will supply nitrogen and other nutrients to encourage good growth (A).

STEP 2 Remove the plants from their small pots and arrange them on the soil surface in the large pot (B). Seven or eight plants will fit snugly in an 18-inch (46-cm) pot. Rather than space the tallest plant in the center, arrange them in an asymmetrical layout (C). That way, as you harvest your greens, the balance of the design will evolve without becoming lopsided.

STEP 3 Surround the transplants with potting soil, firming soil around the roots. Place the pot where it will get at least six hours of sunlight per day.

181 grow self-watering greens

Lettuces and herbs that water themselves are perfect for busy gardeners or those who travel a lot.

MATERIALS

3 self-watering containers

Potting soil

3 six-packs of mixed lettuces and greens

2 pots each of basil, parsley, nasturtiums, calendula, and pansies

Scissors

STEP 1 Follow the directions for setting up self-watering containers. Most have a screen on the bottom and a water reservoir, and some have gauges. Fill the containers with potting soil or the soil mix the manufacturer recommends, taking care not to get soil in the water reservoir (A). Plant the greens, herbs, and flowers.

STEP 3 Water the plants, then fill the water reservoir; if there is a gauge, check the water level and fill to the maximum (B). Depending on weather conditions, you might need to refill the water reservoir every two to seven days.

STEP 4 To harvest greens and flowers, clip them with scissors. Cut outer leaves of lettuces and greens individually, or cut the whole plant at once. Harvest your edible flowers by cutting the stem just below the bloom (C).

182 sow a salad

Planting greens and salad ingredients in accessible pots is easy.

MATERIALS

Bowl-shape pots

Compost-enriched
  potting mix

Trowel

Seeds

Plant labels

Vermiculite

Burlap

STEP 1 Fill containers with compost-enriched potting mix or choose an organic mix. Sprinkle the potting mix with water to moisten it. Sow one seed variety in each container and tuck in a plant label (A).

STEP 2 Following planting directions on the seed packet, cover the seeds with a layer of vermiculite to the depth advised (usually the thickness of the seeds) (B).

STEP 3 Cover the planting with a piece of burlap cut to fit inside the pot. Sprinkle with water until the water runs out the bottom of the pot (C). The vermiculite and the burlap help keep the potting mix evenly damp while the seeds germinate. Peek under the burlap every few days to check the plantings and determine whether watering is needed.

STEP 4 Remove the burlap when the seeds germinate; timing varies according to plant varieties (D). Radishes typically sprout within three days, and other plants sprout within a week or two. Begin harvesting salad ingredients as soon as the leaves or other produce is large enough. Snip herbs, lettuces, and other greens regularly to keep them producing lush new leaves.

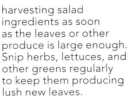

183 garnish grillside

Park a bountiful container of your favorite herbs next to your grill and let the culinary delights roll in.

MATERIALS

Galvanized container

Drill with a ¼-inch (6-mm) bit

Potting soil

Herb plants

STEP 1 Using a drill, create ¼-inch- (6-mm-) diameter drainage holes every 5 inches (13 cm) in the bottom of the galvanized container, drilling from the inside of the container toward the outside to ensure water can easily escape (A).

STEP 2 Fill the container with quality potting soil, which is lightweight, freely draining, and augmented with slow-release nutrients that promote growth all season (B). (Do not use ordinary garden soil in containers. It drains too slowly for a confined environment.) Plant herbs and press soil firmly around the roots.

quick garden tip

184 harvest greens early

Herbs and salad greens are most tender when they're young and small. Harvest young foliage when texture and flavor are best (C).

185 toss a hanging salad

Colorful, curly-edge greens look as pretty in a hanging basket as they do tossed in a salad.

MATERIALS

Hanging basket with a coconut-fiber liner

Potting soil

Fertilizer pellets

Garden scissors or knife

Plant label

6-pack of small lettuce plants

Plastic bag

Two to three 4-inch (10-cm) pots of lettuce plants

Sheet moss

STEP 1 Fill the hanging basket about one-third full of soil. Sprinkle a small handful of fertilizer pellets on top (A).

STEP 2 To plant the sides of the basket, slice or snip a hole in the basket liner at soil level (B). Mark the hole using a plant label.

STEP 3 Choose a small lettuce plant. Cut a piece from the plastic bag and wrap the lettuce leaves, leaving the root ball exposed, to protect the plant as the leaves are forced through the hole. Working from the inside of the basket, poke the wrapped leaves through the hole in the liner, pulling until the leaves come through, with the root ball snug against the inside of the liner (C). Continue planting small lettuces all the way around the sides of the basket.

STEP 4 Fill the basket with soil. Plant larger lettuce plants on top, crowding them in (D).

STEP 5 Place small pieces of sheet moss around the crowns of the lettuce plants (E). Water well, then hang the basket from a sturdy support.

project tip

186 keep greens cool

Most lettuces grow best in slightly cool weather. Plant in early spring or early fall, when most garden shops offer an array of greens.

187 cultivate a good-for-you garden

Get a bumper crop of heart-healthy, antioxidant-rich nutrition from this potted garden.

MATERIALS

28×14×10-inch (70×36×25-cm) terra-cotta pot

Compost-enriched potting mix

Pot feet

Shortcake raspberry

Beet 'Bull's Blood'

Collard

Kale 'Red Russian'

Parsley, flat-leaf Italian

Strawberry

STEP 1 Fill the pot with compost-enriched potting mix. Set the pot on pot feet to allow it to drain freely. Add plants and water thoroughly (A). Water the plants regularly when the soil begins to dry—daily during hot, dry weather.

STEP 2 Plant an everbearing strawberry variety to enjoy a light crop in midsummer and again in late summer. Pinch off any young plants that develop at the end of a long stem or runner to encourage berry production (B).

STEP 3 Snip parsley regularly to keep it growing lush. Harvest the greens—collard and kale—as they mature (C). Hot summer weather causes these cool-season crops to fizzle; remove the spent plants, leaving room for the beets and other plants to grow.

STEP 4 If you live in a cold-winter area, lift the perennial plants—the raspberry (D), strawberry, and parsley—from the pot in late summer or early fall and transplant them into more-permanent places in the garden. Water the plants weekly throughout fall to encourage them to grow new roots and become established before cold weather hits.

project tip

188 harvest antioxidants

Raspberries, strawberries, kale, collard, spinach, beets, and parsley are among the best sources of antioxidants. These plants are all included in this easy-grow container. Choose dwarf plant varieties that are best suited to a small space, and grow this garden of edibles in full sun.

189 grow sweet potatoes in a pot

For one of the easiest-growing crops imaginable, plant sweet potatoes in a pot.

MATERIALS

20-inch- (50-cm-)
 diameter pot

Compost-enriched
 potting mix

Sweet potato plants

STEP 1 Fill the pot with compost-enriched potting mix to within 6 inches (15 cm) of the rim. Snuggle the sweet potato plants into the potting mix, spacing them 9 to 12 inches (23–30 cm) apart and covering the stems up to the bases of the leaves (A). Water after planting and regularly throughout the growing season to keep soil evenly damp.

STEP 2 When the plants begin growing and reaching over the edge of the pot, finish filling the pot with potting mix (B).

STEP 3 Harvest sweet potatoes in early fall before a heavy frost or freeze. Pull the vines out of the containers. Carefully remove the soil and tubers from the pot. Brush off loose soil. Store the tubers (C).

project tip

190 say po-tay-to

Whether you grow ornamental or edible sweet potato vines, the plant is *Ipomoea batatas*, but the cultivars differ. Although the tubers of ornamental varieties, such as 'Blackie' and 'Margarita,' are edible, their flavor is not so good. This warm-weather crop needs a long growing season, from 90 to 140 days, to attain the highest yields.

191 do a hat trick

Combine old-fashioned hats and flowering plants for bonny spring bouquets. Stylish hats might not wield the same fashion power today as they did in 1959, but vintage millinery beauties still have timeless charm—especially when combined with flowers and plants for inventive and simply stunning arrangements. Find mid-century hats at bargain prices in antiques malls, vintage clothing stores, flea markets, and on the internet.

192 fill a bowl with evergreens

A pot of dwarf evergreens brings a tiny woodland scene to your patio.

MATERIALS

14- to 18-inch- (36–46-cm-) diameter low, round planter bowl with drainage hole

Potting mix

2 miniature conifers: 1 tall and columnar and 1 shorter and mounded

5 to 7 interesting stones

Pea gravel

STEP 1 Fill the planter with potting soil to within 2 inches (5 cm) of the rim. Plant the columnar evergreen near one edge of the bowl. Plant the mounding evergreen slightly off center and to one side of the first plant (A). Make sure both plants are planted at the same level as in their nursery pots—neither higher nor lower. Surround the plants with soil, pressing it firmly around the roots. Add or remove soil to create a flat landscape, and press the soil down as you smooth it.

STEP 2 Arrange larger stones on the soil in a natural pattern. When pleased with the placement, press them into the soil ¼ to ½ inch (6–13 mm). Working in small amounts, pour pea gravel on the soil, spreading over the surface and nudging up next to the large stones (B). Place your evergreen bowl in an area that receives at least six hours of direct sunlight daily. Water thoroughly. (In the absence of rain, water once a week, ensuring excess water drains away.) Use a water-soluble fertilizer monthly during the growing season.

A

B

193 design a mossy dish garden

Mound multi-hued and splendidly textured mosses and ferns in a pretty bird bath.

MATERIALS

Safety glasses

Drill and ½-inch (13-mm) drill bit

Ceramic birdbath

Landscape fabric

Pea gravel

Potting soil

Moss and fern plants

Decorative branch

Bamboo skewer or crafts stick

STEP 1 Wearing safety glasses, drill a hole in the center of the birdbath bowl. When drilling, start at an angle to first get a groove, then level the drill and bit to keep the drill from sliding (A). Add a bit of water in the bowl base to cool the heat generated from the drilling. (Or take your birdbath to a tile shop and ask them to drill a hole in the basin for you.)

STEP 2 Line the bowl with landscape fabric to keep soil from plugging the drainage hole. Add a layer of pea gravel on the fabric (B), then add potting soil in a convex shape to allow the moss to mound.

STEP 3 Add moss and fern plants. At about one-third of the diameter inward, place a decorative branch as an accent (C). Continue to add moss and fern plants to cover the soil.

STEP 4 Tuck the moss along the lip of the birdbath bowl (D). We used a bamboo skewer; a crafts stick will also work.

194 get pumped up

Make color pour from the spigot of an old water pump and into a vintage metal bucket overflowing with flowers.

We used Rudbeckia (A), *Pentas* 'New Look White' (B), ornamental pepper (*Capsicum annuum* 'Explosive Ember') (C), ruby grass (*Melinis nerviglumis* 'Pink Crystals') (D), and *Angelonia* 'Serena' (E). Sweet potato vine (*Ipomoea batatas* 'Margarita') spurts out of the pump top. Punch or drill drainage holes into the bottom of the bucket before planting to be sure that excess water flows out.

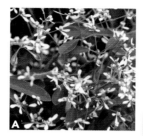

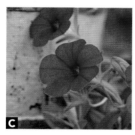

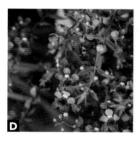

195 make a top-drawer planter

Store vibrant bunches of hardworking annuals in drawers pulled from a salvaged tool chest.

We used *Euphorbia* 'Diamond Frost' (A), Sundaze Flame *Bracteantha bracteata* (B), Superbells Red Calibrachoa hybrid (C), *Angelonia* 'Serena' (D), and *Ipomoea batatas* 'Margarita' (E). Staggering the drawers on three levels of an old stepladder ensures the colorful contents all get sunshine. Soften the base of the ladder with the silvery foliage of lamb's-ears (*Stachys byzantina*).

196 hang blossoming baskets

Turn the purpose of vintage garden tools on end with tools by standing them up as charming garden supports.

Dangling from curlicued copper wire, wooden berry baskets lined with sphagnum moss burst with *Pentas* 'New Look White' (A); ornamental peppers (*Capsicum annuum* 'Red Missile') and Euphorbia 'Diamond Frost' (B); *Capsicum annuum* 'Explosive Ember' (C); and Prelude Scarlet begonia (*Begonia semperflorens*) (D).

197 scoop up some blooms

When a metal grain scoop is no longer used to serve Bessie her supper in the barn, use it to dish up a delectable mix of flowers.

We perched it atop a farm drainage tile posing as a post. Plant pots to place in the scoop. We used Superbells Blue Calibrachoa hybrid (A); *Melampodium* (B); *Nemesia* (C); and *Euphorbia* 'Diamond Frost' and sweet potato vine (*Ipomoea batatas* 'Blackie') (D).

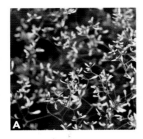

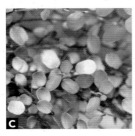

198 flower a chicken feeder

Even flowers have a pecking order. Some are destined to high places; others prefer to keep a low profile. The living proof of this grows in this chicken-feeder container garden.

Euphorbia 'Diamond Frost' (A), Toffee Twist Sedge (*Carex flagellifera*) (B), and creeping wirevine (*Muehlenbeckia*) (C) softly spray out of the top. Hens-and-chicks (*Sempervivum tectorum* 'Silverine') (D) play ring-around-the-rosy in the circular feeding trough below.

199 brighten up a wall

Even gangly tomatoes look lovely when they're surrounded by pretty flowers and suspended from a wrought-iron wall hanger. Partially fill a 30-inch (76-cm) wire window box lined with a coconut-fiber liner with potting mix. Set the tomato plant in the middle with a black-eyed Susan on each side. Set the other plants in place through the holes in the side of the planter and liner. Add more potting mix to cover the root balls of the plants. Set two *Melampodium* on each end. Fill in with potting mix.

A. Tomato 'Husky Cherry Red'
B. Black-eyed Susan (*Rudbeckia*)
C. *Melampodium* **D.** Wax begonia (*B. semperflorens*) **E.** Globe amaranth (*Gomphrena*) **F.** Creeping Jenny (*Lysimachia* 'Aurea')

200 ascend a floral flight of drawers

With minimal carpentry, flea-market dresser drawers become a showplace staircase planter.

MATERIALS:

4 equal-size drawers

Disposable gloves

Spray paint (for hardware)

1 quart (1 L) exterior latex paint

Paintbrush

Tape measure

Carpenters square

Two 6-foot (1.8-m) 1×12 boards (for the stair stringers)

Circular saw

Handsaw

Drill and bits

Two 8-foot (2.5-m) 2×4 boards cut in the following pieces: two 3-foot (1-m) lengths; two 10½-inch (27-cm) lengths; one 13½-inch (34-cm) length

Clamps

2-inch (5-cm) No. 8 screws

1½-inch (4-cm) No. 6 screws

Potting soil

Plants

STEP 1 Remove the hardware from your drawers and, wearing disposable gloves, spray-paint the pieces. Paint the drawers inside and out with several coats of latex paint, dabbing paint well into the corners to protect the drawers from weather. Let dry between coats (A).

STEP 2 Measure the drawers. (Our drawers are 16×11½×6 inches [40×29×15 cm]. We designed a stringer with 9-inch [23-cm] risers and 9-inch [23-cm] treads for the drawers to overlap each other a little. Our planter is 3 feet [1 m] tall and 15 inches [38 cm] wide.) Lay the carpenters square on a 1×12 board with the corner pointing toward the center of the board. (For our planter, we aligned the 9-inch [23-cm] marks along the edge of the board to create 9-inch [23-cm] risers and treads.) Draw lines along the outside edges of the carpenters square (B). This 90-degree angle marks one riser and one tread. Slide the carpenters square over and repeat, marking another 90-degree angle. Repeat until you have outlined four steps. Do the same on the remaining 1×12 for a matching stringer.

STEP 3 Using a circular saw, cut along the marked lines on each stringer (C). To get clean corners, finish the cuts with the handsaw. Finish the ends of each stringer with a 90-degree cut.

STEP 4 Make a back support. Drill pilot holes 3 inches (8 cm) from the ends of each 3-foot (1-m) 2×4. Join both 3-foot (1-m) lengths with a 10½-inch (27-cm) length placed perpendicular between them at either end, using No. 8 screws (D).

STEP 5 Prop the stringers against the back support, clamp in place, and attach each stringer with three 2-inch (5-cm) No. 8 screws (E).

STEP 6 Attach the 13½-inch (34-cm) 2×4 between stringers, level with the bottom tread, driving two No. 8 screws into each end (F). Paint the stairs; let dry. Screw the drawers to the stringers with the No. 6 screws. Drill four ½-inch (1.25-cm) holes in the bottom of each drawer for drainage. Fill the drawers with potting soil and plants.

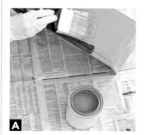
A

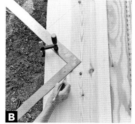
B

C

D

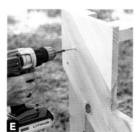
E

F

201 shadow-box with flowers

This pretty-as-a-picture planter mimics a tiny theater where miniature plants play starring roles.

MATERIALS

8-foot (2.5-m) 1×6 cedar board, cut into the following pieces: two 16-inch (40-cm) lengths (sides); two 10¾-inch (27.5-cm) lengths (top and bottom); two 14½-inch (37-cm) lengths (back)

Exterior latex paint in two colors

2-inch- (5-cm-) wide paintbrush

Drill and drill bit

1¼-inch (3-cm) No. 8 screws

Scissors

Plastic-mesh gutter guard

Staple gun

Hammer

Sheet moss

Potting soil

Assorted plants

STEP 1 Paint the cedar boards. If you use rough cedar, rough sides will go toward the inside of the shadow box. Paint the rough sides one color (we chose yellow) and the smooth sides another color (we chose blue). One coat is enough. Let dry several hours (A).

STEP 2 To construct the box, form a butt joint by placing the side pieces against the bottom. Drill two screws through each side into the bottom piece (B). Fit the two back boards into the shadow box to rest on the bottom board. Set the top board in place; drill two screws through each side into an end of the top board. To secure the back, drill two screws into the top and two through the bottom into the back pieces.

STEP 3 Cut a 1-foot (30-cm) length of gutter guard and stretch it across the bottom front of the shadow box. Attach the gutter guard using a staple gun; hammer the staples to secure (C).

STEP 4 Soak the sheet moss in water until spongy and pliable. Squeeze gently and tuck it in the box up against the gutter guard (D). Fill the area behind the sheet moss half-full with potting soil.

STEP 5 Add both trailing and upright plants for depth and dimension (E). Contrasting colors and variegated plants will stand out nicely. Fill in with extra potting soil and moss as needed.

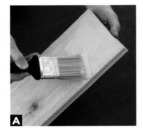
A

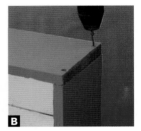
B

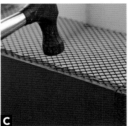
C

D

E

---

project tip

202 dig up sheet moss

Find sheet moss at garden shops. When you buy dried moss it is brittle, but soaking it in water for a few minutes rehydrates the moss and makes it pliable. Press bits of moist moss together for seamless coverage of the gutter guard.

203 create a peekaboo planter

Like a molded sugar peekaboo Easter egg with a tiny spring scene inside, this planter houses a treasure of wee plants, moss, and artificial mushrooms.

MATERIALS:

Burlap

14-inch- (36-cm-) diameter grapevine wreath form

Scissors

Moisture-retentive liner

Potting mix

Plants: *Lysimachia congestiflora* 'Variegated,' maidenhair fern 'Bronze Venus' (*Adiantum hispidulum*), *Lamiastrum* 'Hermann's Pride,' aluminum plant (*Pilea cadierei*), fern 'Fluffy Ruffle' (*Nephrolepis exaltata*), and begonia 'Lucky Strike'

Preserved moss

Artificial mushrooms or other garden accents

STEP 1 Cut burlap to line the bottom third of the wreath form (A).

STEP 2 Cut the moisture-retentive liner slightly smaller than the burlap; place it on the burlap (B). Sprinkle enough potting mix to just cover them.

STEP 3 Unpot the plants and set them inside the wreath form in a pleasing design—tallest ones to the sides and cascading plants along the front edge. Fill gaps and cover roots with potting mix (C).

STEP 4 Moisten the preserved moss in a container of water. Remove a handful of moss and squeeze out excess water. Cover the plant root balls and any exposed soil with moss (D). Finish by tucking in artificial mushrooms or other garden accents.

A

B

C

D

204 make a tiny fish pond

Enjoy the cool touch this quick-as-a-wink water garden brings to an outdoor space.

MATERIALS

Large glass container (we used a 3-gallon [11.5-L] apothecary jar)

Large rocks

Water

Aquarium water conditioner

2 water hyacinth plants

1 water lettuce plant

Thermometer

1 goldfish or minnow

STEP 1 Cover the bottom of the glass container with one or more large rocks, which are easier to remove for cleaning than gravel or pebbles (A). (Or omit the rocks.)

STEP 2 Fill the container with clean water to within 2 inches (5 cm) of the top and let the water come to ambient temperature. (Or let the water stand for 24 hours.) If adding fish, pour in a few drops of aquarium water conditioner to remove chlorine and chloramines (B).

STEP 3 Add the water hyacinths and water lettuce, spreading the roots so they float beneath the surface (C).

STEP 4 If adding a fish, use a thermometer to check the water temperature. Most fish prefer water between 70 and 80°F (21–27°C). Add fish slowly, tipping the bag or container gently into the water garden to mix the waters. A single fish will do fine—the general rule is no more than 1 inch (2.5 cm) of fish per 1 square foot (930 sq cm) of water.

A

B

C

205 sculpt a wire accent

Obelisks shaped from boldly colored wire create dramatic planter accents.

MATERIALS

150-grit sandpaper

9½-inch (24-cm) resin urn

13-inch (33-cm) resin pot

Paintbrush

Exterior acrylic paint in gold and copper metallic

Rag

Potting mix

Lysimachia 'Walkabout Sunset'

Begonia 'Lois Burks'

Wire cutters

Strong and malleable 6-gauge aluminum wire in gold and copper

Floral clay

Copper plumbing reducer

STEP 1 Lightly sand the resin pots, sanding more in some spots and less in others. Barely dip a dry paintbrush into the metallic paint, then dab off excess on a rag. Lightly brush the gold paint on a small area of a pot, then dab the paint with a rag. Continue painting and dabbing until the entire pot is covered (A). Repeat with copper paint and the other pot. Let dry.

STEP 2 Fill each pot three-quarters full with potting mix. Add plants, and fill in around them with potting mix (B). Water thoroughly.

STEP 3 Cut 4 to 6 pieces of the aluminum wire the same length for each pot. Bend them into matching shapes, such as simple arches (C).

STEP 4 For the gold-wire obelisk: Insert one end of the wire into the potting soil and bend it across the pot, inserting the opposite end into the soil on the other side. Repeat around the pot. For the copper-wire obelisk: Evenly space the shaped wires around the pot, pressing them into the potting mix. Gather the loose ends in the center.

STEP 5 To finish the copper-wire obelisk, roll a 2-inch (5-cm) piece of floral clay and press it into the plumbing reducer. Push the clay-filled copper piece over the gathered ends to hold wires in place (D).

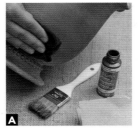

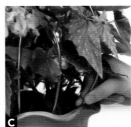

206 discover the fountain of mirth

Sit back and enjoy the kinetic art of water bubbling in a beautiful fountain. A small water feature such as this do-it-yourself fountain has the advantage of a water garden with little maintenance, creating a peaceful setting and attracting wildlife. For this weekend project, you'll need a watertight urn, a preformed pond liner/reservoir, a submersible pump, a sturdy grate to cover the reservoir, and fountain tubing. Also round up silicone sealant, concrete half-blocks, and stones. Excavate an area to accommodate the pond liner. Set the pump in the reservoir; nestle concrete blocks around the pump to secure it and provide a sturdy base for the urn. Extend a length of fountain tubing from the top of the urn down through its drainage hole and extending at least 1 to 2 feet (30–60 cm). Use waterproof silicone to seal around the tubing inside and outside the urn. Let the sealant dry. Feed the fountain tubing through the center of the grate, and attach it to the top of the pump. Set the grate over the reservoir; stand the urn on the grate, centered over the pump. Cover the grate with stones. Fill the reservoir with water. Plug the pump into a GFCI outlet.

207 salvage a window box

A mix of rustic farmhouse elements—galvanized pails and hen nesters, a calf bucket, and shelf brackets—ensures this project has funky flair.

MATERIALS

Tape measure

Galvanized hen nester or other approximately 3×1-foot (90×30-cm) tray with 2-inch- (5-cm-) tall sides

Pencil

3 galvanized shelf brackets to support a 1-foot- (30-cm-) wide shelf

Drill

2½-inch (6.5-cm) wood screws (the type of mounting hardware might vary depending on your home's siding)

⅜×¾-inch (10×19-mm) bolts with washers and nuts to fit

Burlap to cover the bottom of the tray

Potting soil

2 galvanized pails

Galvanized calf bucket

Vintage outdoor faucet handle

Instant glue

Perennials or annuals (we used Shasta daisies, *Vinca major*, and dwarf gerbera daisies)

Succulents (we used hens-and-chicks, echeveria, sedum, and *Bacopa*)

STEP 1 Measure the length of the tray or hen nester. Mark the locations for the brackets on the siding of the house (A).

STEP 2 The bracket supporting each end of the shelf should be 3 inches (8 cm) from the edge of the tray. Predrill holes for the screws (B).

STEP 3 Attach each bracket to the siding with three 2½-inch (6.5-cm) wood screws (C).

STEP 4 Place the hen nester or tray on the brackets and attach it to the brackets with bolts, washers, and nuts (D).

STEP 5 Blanket the bottom of the tray or nester with burlap to prevent the potting soil from washing out of the tray's mesh or drainage holes (E).

STEP 6 Cover the tray bottom with a 2-inch- (5-cm) thick layer of potting soil (F).

STEP 7 Drill three ¼-inch (6-mm) drainage holes in each pail and calf bucket bottom (G). Attach a vintage faucet handle to the calf bucket handle with instant glue.

STEP 8 Fill the containers with potting soil. Add favorite annuals or perennials, such as Shasta daisies, *Vinca major*, and dwarf gerbera daisies.

STEP 9 Finish the planting tray with a selection of succulents (I). Hens-and-chicks, echeveria, sedum, and *Bacopa* work nicely. Water well.

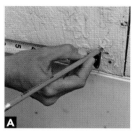

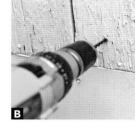

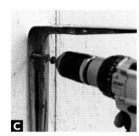

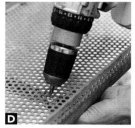

208 make a hypertufa trough

Show off your favorite plants in a homemade artificial-stone container.

MATERIALS

Tape measure or ruler

Marker

Serrated knife

2-inch- (5-cm-) thick foam insulation

Eight 3¼-inch (8.25-cm) nails

Tape

Rubber or latex gloves

Portland cement

Perlite

Peat moss

1-gallon (3.75-L) container (for measurement)

Wheelbarrow

Hoe

Reinforced concrete fibers

Warm water

2×2-foot (60×60-cm) piece of ⅜-inch- (1-cm-) thick plywood

Spray bottle of water

½-inch (1.25-cm) dowel

Wire brush or screwdriver (optional)

STEP 1 Measure and use a serrated knife to cut the insulation into two 16×6-inch (40×15-cm) pieces and two 18×6-inch (46×15-cm) pieces. Position them to make a rectangular mold for the trough. Insert two nails through each corner—one at the top and one at the bottom (A).

STEP 2 Wrap the tape two times around your mold, once near the top and once near the bottom, for added reinforcement (B).

STEP 3 Mark a line at least 2 inches (5 cm) from the mold's bottom as a guide for the depth of the hypertufa; this will be the thickness of the bottom of the trough (C). (If you make a larger container, form a deeper layer of hypertufa for more support.)

STEP 4 Put on gloves and measure 2 gallons (7.5 L) cement, 2 gallons (7.5 L) perlite, and 4 gallons (15 L) peat moss. (The leftover makes trough feet.) Mix dry ingredients in a wheelbarrow with the hoe. Add ⅓ cup (80 mL) of reinforced concrete fibers for more strength.

STEP 5 Slowly add warm water to the wheelbarrow (D). Start with about 3 gallons (11.5 L) and mix it well with the dry materials until your mixture resembles cookie dough. It should be wet enough to hold together when compressed but not ooze water (E). Set the mold on the plywood.

STEP 6 Pack the mixture onto the mold bottom up to the marked line. Work a small area at a time; firmly press the mixture into the bottom corners and up the sides. Mash one section into another. Continue up the sides until the mold's inside is covered by a 2-inch- (5-cm-) thick layer (F). Spray with water as needed while working.

STEP 7 To provide proper drainage, use a dowel to poke holes in the bottom of the trough (G). Insert the dowel through the hypertufa until it meets the plywood base, making six evenly spaced holes. Use the leftover mixture to create feet. Let the trough dry in a protected spot for 48 hours.

STEP 8 Carefully remove the tape and nails once it's dry; remove the mold (H). For a textured look, gently score the exterior with a wire brush or screwdriver. Store in a shady area to cure for 30 to 60 days. Spray with water often. The trough can be left out in freezing temperatures if off the ground.

A

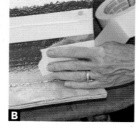
B

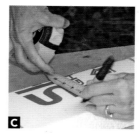
C

D

E

F

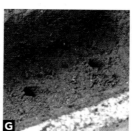
G

H

209 pipe up with planters

Make garden borders more assertive with a crescendo of succulents.

MATERIALS

10-foot (3-m) length of 4-inch- (10-cm-) diameter PVC pipe

Circular saw or hacksaw

Metal file

Universal-bonding primer spray paint

Hammered spray paint, copper

Shovel

Potting mix

Assorted succulents

STEP 1 Cut the PVC pipe into varying lengths using a circular saw. We cut lengths of 8 to 18 inches (20–46 cm) (A).

STEP 2 Use a metal file to smooth the cut edges (B).

STEP 3 Coat the pipes with primer spray paint to help the copper-color spray paint adhere to the smooth surfaces. Let dry. Using long, even strokes, spray the pipes with hammered copper paint; let dry (C).

STEP 4 Dig a trench 4 inches (10 cm) deep at the site of your border (D).

STEP 5 Position the pipes in the trench and pack soil around each base to hold the pipes straight. Fill each pipe with potting soil to within 4 inches (10 cm) of the top (E). Plant the succulents in the pipes, filling any gaps with more potting soil. Water the succulents thoroughly. Although succulents are drought-hardy, they need about 1 inch (2.5 cm) of water weekly.

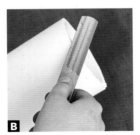

210 add a touch of farmhouse chic

Add a secluded hideout to your patio with two planters made from metal livestock water tanks.

MATERIALS

Drill and ½-inch (13-mm) cobalt bit

88-gallon (3.3-hL) galvanized stock tank

169-gallon (6.4-hL) galvanized stock tank

Gloves

30 cubic feet (0.8 cbm) of raised bed potting soil

3 hibiscus plants (Summerific 'Cherry Cheesecake')

5 variegated cannas ('Pretoria' and 'Tropicana Gold')

STEP 1 Using a ½-inch (13-mm) cobalt bit, drill six to eight evenly spaced holes across the bottom of each tank for drainage (A).

STEP 2 Wearing gloves, fill each tank three-fourths full with potting soil (B). (We used a mix specifically designed for raised beds.)

STEP 3 Remove the plants from their plastic pots and place them in the tanks, spacing them a little more tightly than recommended on their tags (C). We planted hibiscuses and cannas roughly 10 inches (25 cm) apart. Water thoroughly.

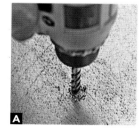

211 craft a planter from a rain gutter

Perfect for a balcony railing, this mod planter is made from a highly utilitarian product.

MATERIALS

Tape measure

Tin snips

Galvanized gutter (typically sold in 10-foot [3 m] lengths)

2 gutter end caps (one left, one right)

Rubber mallet

Pliers

Construction adhesive

Drill and drill bits

Wood screws

Potting soil

Pumice

Mixed succulents in 4-inch (10-cm) pots

STEP 1 Measure and use tin snips to cut the gutter to your preferred length, then add end caps. Fit the end caps to their respective ends of the gutter and tap into place with a rubber mallet. Use pliers to pinch the end cap edges securely over the gutter edges. Following the package instructions, apply the construction adhesive along the inside seams where the end caps and gutter meet. Let the glue set.

STEP 2 Drill holes every 4 inches (10 cm) along the bottom of the gutter for drainage. Drill mounting holes at the top back of the gutter: one at each end and one every 1 foot (30 cm). Holding the gutter in position, mark mounting points on the deck railing; drill pilot holes. Securely fasten the gutter to the railing with wood screws.

STEP 3 Mix 2 parts potting soil and 1 part pumice together in a bucket. Fill the mounted gutter with this lightweight, well-draining planting mix. Remove the plants from their pots, loosen their root balls, and plant them in the gutter. Fill any gaps with small divisions of groundcover sedums and hens-and-chicks for a solid tapestry of shapes, colors, and textures. Water the finished planting to settle roots and soil.

project tip

212 play it safe

When you're cutting metal (as in the planter project above), you risk cuts from very sharp edges and eye injuries from flying bits of metal as you cut. Wear protective gloves and glasses to avoid a trip to the emergency room.

213 wrap up a birch-bark pot

Bring ephemeral beauty into your landscape with an easy-to-make woodland-inspired container.

MATERIALS

Terra-cotta container

Heavy-duty scissors

Sheets of bark

Twine or string

Potting soil

Wildflowers or plants

STEP 1 Select a container large enough to hold your plants.

STEP 2 Using heavy-duty scissors, cut the bark a bit taller than the pot and long enough to overlap the ends when wrapped around it (A). Tie twine to secure the bark (B).

STEP 3 Combine several compatible wildflowers or other plants in the pot. When they finish flowering, plant them in your garden for the following year (C).

project tip

214 transplant properly

Growing woodland plants or wildflowers in containers provides a later opportunity for you to transplant them into your garden. Most woodland plants prefer dappled sun or shade and thrive in relatively moist soil that is rich in organic material.

A

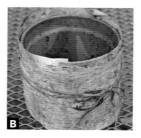

B

C

215 plant your porch

Bring your porch to life with shade-loving houseplants, shrubs, and colorful annuals.

CHOOSE SUCCULENTS
With a simple weekly water requirement and tolerance of various light levels, succulents are a smart addition to any porch. This collection of petite succulents (A) is planted in a cast-off basket—so easy!

PLANT IN PLASTIC Make the annual transition from indoors to outdoors easy by planting houseplants in plastic pots that can be placed in hefty ceramic, stone, or wood exterior pots (B). It is much easier to tote a plastic pot indoors and outdoors than a heavy and unwieldy ceramic container complete with a thriving houseplant.

LINE HANGING BASKETS
Hanging planter baskets are must-have elements of a lush porch, but winds tend to quickly dry the soil in the porous containers. To reduce watering chores, line the baskets with plastic (C). Punch several holes in the bottom of the plastic lining to ensure excess water will escape.

216 roll with it

Move retired garden gear out of the shed and into the spotlight as clever vessels for potted plants. Wagons and wheelbarrows steal the show when piled high with beautiful plantings. You don't even need a coat of paint to breathe fresh life into cast-off haulers. All it takes is an eye for color and a passion for plants. Some plants—such as the coleus, purple Persian shield, *Dichondra argentea* 'Silver Falls,' blue-purple Torenia, and Tiger Eyes sumac shown here—bring panache to any container garden.

217 cultivate feng shui

Three stalks of lucky bamboo in a harmonious arrangement are sure to inspire peace and tranquility.

MATERIALS

Pruning shears or flower snips

3 stalks of lucky bamboo (*Dracaena sanderiana*)

Small red vase

Small clean pebbles

Wood tray

Several large pebbles

Metal goldfish figurine

STEP 1 Cut the lucky bamboo stems into three different lengths, making the longest stems about 2½ times the height of the vase (A).

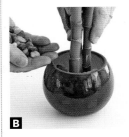

STEP 2 Arrange your bamboo in a cluster at the center of the vase. Pour small pebbles around the base of the stems, filling the vase nearly to the top (B). Add fresh water to just below the top of the pebbles.

STEP 3 Place the vase at one end of the tray. Arrange the remaining small and large pebbles on the tray, and position the goldfish among the pebbles (C). Place the arrangement in bright, indirect light. Drain the water every two weeks and replace with fresh water.

---

project tip

218 know your "bamboo"

Although it is somewhat similar in appearance to bamboo, lucky bamboo is actually *Dracaena sanderiana*, a native of West Africa. It's shaped by twisting and looping the stems when they are young and slender. If potted in pebbles and water, as shown in this project, change the water completely every two weeks, and add liquid fertilizer for aquatic plants.

219 create a patio pond

Make this patio or deck-top pond in an afternoon. Start with a watertight container that's at least 1 foot (30 cm) in diameter and has at least a 5-gallon (19-L) capacity—twice that size works even better. Cover the soil of potted water garden plants, such as dwarf hardy water lily and taro, with a layer of nonlimestone gravel; set the potted plants on the bottom of the container. Fill the container with water and drop in water lettuce. Add nontoxic mosquito control product to prevent larvae from developing, or add a submersible pump with an attached fountainhead to keep the water moving and minimize mosquitoes.

four ways to shape tiny trees

Shapely topiaries made from small trees or tree-form plants create bold and artful effects—in your garden or in your home—while extending the longevity of the potted plants.

220 contour coleus

A small-leaf coleus (*Solenostemon scutellarioides* 'Mars') shapes up into a simple geometric topiary form that overwinters indoors. Various perennials, herbs, trees, and shrubs prove suitable for topiary forms if they grow from a central stem and have compact, dense foliage.

221 shape cypress

Pint-size Italian cypresses (*Cupressus sempervirens*) suit small-space gardens with their slow-growing tree forms that need no shearing to remain shapely. Let all topiaries rest in the winter; lay off clipping and fertilizing until spring. Water topiaries regularly to keep soil from drying out. Feed the plants monthly throughout the growing season.

222 wind up ivy

Ivy needs little encouragement to find its way around a wire topiary form. You might want to start with a ready-made topiary and let the cuts made at the nursery be your guide to trimming. Use floral scissors or pruners to trim plants.

223 have a ball

Trailing sedum foliage softens the formality of sweet myrtle topiary balls planted in terra-cotta pots. Pairing tree-form plants doubles their impact. When training a new topiary, select a plant with a strong central stem. For a ball shape atop a main stem, start by pruning the lower branches to reveal the stem.

224 bring a sea breeze to your backyard

The look of driftwood and beachy grasses in this planter shore up a coastal theme.

MATERIALS

- Small paint-mixing bucket and stirrer
- Primer
- Water
- One bundle 18-inch (46-cm) hand-split cedar shingles (enough to cover 15 square feet [1.5 sq m])
- Newspapers
- Disposable gloves
- 3-inch (8-cm) disposable paintbrush
- Cotton paint rags
- Multisurface outdoor construction adhesive and caulk gun
- Three 14-inch- (36-cm-) square, 8-gallon (30-L) plastic planters
- 3 large potted ornamental grasses (we used *Miscanthus sinensis*)

STEP 1 In the small paint-mixing bucket, combine 1 cup (240 mL) primer with 4 cups (1 L) water. Lay the cedar shingles out on newspapers, rough side up. Wearing gloves, quickly brush diluted primer on three shingles at a time (A). Move on to Step 2 immediately.

STEP 2 Using a cotton rag, wipe the wet primer solution off the surface of the shingles, leaving a light layer of primer that settles into the grain of the wood (B). Continue with remaining shingles, three at a time. Let the shingles dry completely.

STEP 3 Follow the instructions printed on the construction adhesive and make sure the planter and the shingles are free from dust or grease. Choose three or four shingles to fit along one side of the planter, planning placement before you begin. In some cases, overlap shingles or split them lengthwise to get a good fit and appearance. Apply a thick bead of construction adhesive along the top edge of the planter, then put your shingles in place—primed side out—and press them onto the side of the planter (C). If shingles overlap, apply adhesive where they touch. Apply shingles to the planter's other three sides, then allow it to stand for several hours or overnight before moving on to Step 4. Repeat on all planters.

STEP 4 Lay each planter on one side and apply the adhesive, securing your shingles to each other and the planter around the bottom edge (D). Allow the adhesive to dry overnight.

STEP 5 Plant the grasses in the planters (E), adding soil as needed, and water thoroughly.

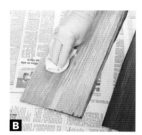

A

B

C

D

E

project tip

225 go with grasses

Choose grasses that can tolerate colder weather than you experience in your area. Unpot the grass and divide every few years to keep it looking its best. Let the grass grow all summer and enjoy the texture through the winter.

226 bring on fragrant narcissus

Paperwhite narcissus (Narcissus papyraceus) bulbs require neither soil nor prechilling for forcing.

STEP 1 Start bulbs anytime from early fall to midwinter for blooming within three to six weeks. Use a container that holds a single bulb or a handful. Plant paperwhites in a potting medium of pebbles, glass marbles, sand, or potting mix. Multiple containers grown at intervals create an ongoing display of intensely scented flowers.

STEP 2 Cover 2 to 3 inches (5–8 cm) of the bottom of a watertight container with gravel. (You can substitute potting mix for gravel if desired.) Snuggle the narcissus bulb bases into the pebbles, pointed ends facing up.

STEP 3 Cover the bulbs up to the necks with pebbles. The tips of the bulbs should remain above the gravel. Add enough water to reach the bottom of the bulbs—about 1 inch (2.5 cm) deep in gravel or until the potting mix is moistened. To maximize blooms, set the container in a cool 40 to 60°F (4–16°C) place with bright light.

227 start seeds in style

Upcycle newspapers into funky, budget-friendly pots for starting herb and flower seeds.

MATERIALS

Newspaper (cut to size)

Jar

Pan

Seed-starting (soilless) potting mix

Seeds

Vermiculite

Wood labels

Plastic wrap

Heating pad

STEP 1 Immerse rectangles of newspaper, sized to wrap around a small jar, in a pan of water until moistened. Roll the softened paper around the jar, extending the bottom edge enough to enfold the bottom (A).

STEP 2 Crimp and press the paper around the bottom of the jar. Flatten the bottom by pressing it on a flat surface. Carefully slide the paper pot off the jar, and set it aside to dry overnight (B).

STEP 3 Stand the paper pots in a pan. Fill them with moistened soilless seed-starting mix, and then plant your seeds according to the directions on the seed packets. Cover the seeds with vermiculite; sprinkle with warm water. Label your plantings (C).

STEP 4 Cover the paper pots with plastic wrap to retain moisture. Set the pan on a heating pad (D) until the seeds sprout, then remove the plastic wrap. Place your seedlings under grow lights for between 14 and 16 hours a day to harden them and ready them for transplant.

A

B

C

D

index

weldon**owen**

PRESIDENT & PUBLISHER	Roger Shaw
SVP, SALES & MARKETING	Amy Kaneko
SENIOR EDITOR	Lucie Parker
EDITORIAL ASSISTANT	Molly O'Neil Stewart
CREATIVE DIRECTOR	Kelly Booth
ART DIRECTOR	Lorraine Rath
ASSOCIATE PRODUCTION DIRECTOR	Michelle Duggan
IMAGING MANAGER	Don Hill

Waterbury Publications, Inc.

CREATIVE DIRECTOR	Ken Carlson
EDITORIAL DIRECTOR	Lisa Kingsley
SENIOR EDITOR	Tricia Bergman
ART DIRECTOR	Doug Samuelson
PRODUCTION ASSISTANT	Mindy Samuelson

Meredith Core Media

EDITORIAL CONTENT DIRECTOR	Doug Kouma
BRAND LEADER	Karman Hotchkiss
CREATIVE DIRECTOR	Michelle Bilyeu
Business Administration	
VICE PRESIDENT/GROUP PUBLISHER	Scott Mortimer
EXECUTIVE ACCOUNT DIRECTOR	Doug Stark

All content and images courtesy of Meredith Corporation with exception of the following:

Shutterstock: 006, 022, 025, 028, 040, 046, 048, 050, 055, 057, 065, 067, 073, 074 (second page of steps: starter plant, trowel, and terra-cotta planter pot), 077, 081, 083, 091, 093, 095, Inviting Wildlife opener, 098 (F, I), 100, 119 (B, F, H, I, J, full-page opposite: hummingbird), 122, 123, 135, 151, 166, 179 (main image: popcorn in pan and corn), 186, 188, 190, 202, 212, 225

© 2017 Weldon Owen Inc.
1045 Sansome Street
San Francisco, CA 94111
www.weldonowen.com

Weldon Owen is a division of Bonnier Publishing USA.

Library of Congress Control Number is on file with the publisher.

ISBN 978-168188-287-1

10 9 8 7 6 5 4 3 2 1

2017 2018 2019 2020 2021

Printed in China.